CHITCHAT CHRONICLES

A Beginner's Guide to Mandarin Chinese with Short Stories and Accent Mastery

Zhang Y. Hua

ISBN-13: 9798858263470

ISBN-10: 1477123456

Cover design by: Art Painter

Library of Congress Control Number: 2018675309

Printed in the United States of America

DEDICATION

To all language enthusiasts, adventurers of the mind, and those who believe in the magic of communication,

This book is dedicated to you. May these Chitchat Chronicles be your gateway to the captivating world of Mandarin Chinese. Just as each character and tone weaves a tapestry of meaning, may your journey through these pages unravel the beauty and depth of a language that bridges cultures and hearts.

May the short stories within spark your imagination and kindle your passion for learning. Let these tales not only teach you words, but also transport you to new horizons, where understanding blossoms and connections flourish.

Accent mastery, like a musical note, carries the melody of a language. May the guidance offered here help you dance with the tones and rhythms of Mandarin, turning every interaction into a symphony of harmony.

As you embark on this linguistic expedition, remember that every word learned, every sentence formed, brings you closer to the world and its people. Embrace the challenge, relish the progress, and let the art of Chitchat lead you to fluency.

With boundless excitement,

Zhang Y. Hua

PREFACE

Welcome to the Chitchat Chronicles, a whimsical and practical journey into the captivating world of Mandarin Chinese. Imagine standing at the threshold of a linguistic adventure where each character, each tone, and every story is a key to unlock new dimensions of communication and culture.

In these pages, we invite you to embark on a voyage that blends the joy of storytelling with the art of language acquisition. Here, you'll not only learn the foundations of Mandarin Chinese but also immerse yourself in short stories that transport you from ancient tea gardens to bustling modern cities.

But the Chitchat Chronicles are more than just stories and vocabulary. They are a guide to mastering accents, those subtle brushstrokes that paint the canvas of speech. We understand that tackling tones might feel like navigating a maze at first, but fear not! With our unique approach, you'll soon find yourself waltzing through the melodies of Mandarin.

So, whether you're a language enthusiast, a traveler, or simply someone seeking new horizons, join us in unraveling the linguistic tapestry of Mandarin Chinese. Let the Chitchat Chronicles be your lantern, illuminating the path to linguistic fluency while nurturing your curiosity and love for language.

Get ready to unlock the magic of Mandarin, one chitchat at a time.

Happy learning!

Zhang Y. Hua

CONTENTS

INTRODUCTION
Embarking on a Linguistic Odyssey with Chitchat Chronicles

In the boundless tapestry of human expression, language stands as a masterpiece, weaving connections between cultures, transcending barriers, and revealing the kaleidoscope of human experience. At the heart of this intricate web lies Mandarin Chinese, a language that holds the key to an ancient civilization's wisdom and a modern global powerhouse's dynamism. Welcome, intrepid reader, to a transformative journey through the Chitchat Chronicles: A Beginner's Guide to Mandarin Chinese with Short Stories and Accent Mastery.

Unveiling the Tapestry

In the pages that follow, you are invited to embark on a voyage that intertwines the art of language acquisition with the enchantment of storytelling. Imagine delving into a world where each character is a brushstroke, every tone a musical note, and each phrase a gateway to a rich cultural landscape. The Chitchat Chronicles beckon you to explore not merely words on paper but the very essence of Mandarin Chinese itself.

A Symphony of Stories

Language is the heartbeat of culture, and stories are the vessels that carry its pulse through time. Within these Chronicles, you will encounter a collection of short stories that span centuries and continents. You'll wander through ancient courtyards, bustling markets, and serene gardens, as these tales unravel the threads of tradition, wisdom, and human connection. From mythic legends to everyday anecdotes, these stories aren't confined by their words; they are bridges to a tapestry were language blooms into life.

Navigating the Tonescape

Yet, mastering Mandarin isn't a mere exercise in vocabulary; it's a symphony of tones, a melody of accents that infuse your words with meaning. We acknowledge the challenge that these tonal intricacies present, and within the Chitchat Chronicles, you will discover a guiding light. Through ingenious exercises and insights, you will find yourself navigating the labyrinth of tones with newfound confidence. Like a composer creating a masterpiece, you will gradually blend pronunciation, rhythm, and expression into a harmonious ensemble.

From Novice to Connoisseur

Whether you're a linguistics enthusiast, a traveler preparing for a cross-cultural adventure, or simply a curious soul craving intellectual exploration, the Chitchat Chronicles are tailored to your individual journey. This book is more than a guide; it is a companion that celebrates your progress, challenges your intellect, and empowers your linguistic evolution. With each chapter, you'll embrace the language's intricacies, drawing closer to fluency while savoring every step of the way.

An Invitation to Immerse

The Chitchat Chronicles extend an invitation, not just to read, but to immerse yourself in a dynamic learning experience. As you progress through the pages, you'll encounter exercises that encourage you to engage actively with the language. You'll transcribe characters, replicate tones, and construct sentences that gradually evolve from learned constructs to intuitive communication. This journey isn't just about mastering a new skill; it's about cultivating a deep understanding of the interplay between words, culture, and human connection.

Your Companion for Discovery

Consider the Chitchat Chronicles your steadfast companion as you embark on this linguistic expedition. Together, we'll traverse the fascinating landscapes of Mandarin Chinese, venturing beyond textbooks and classrooms into a realm where language pulsates with life. Whether you're studying solo or engaging in lively con versations with fellow learners, the Chronicles will be by your side, a source of guidance and inspiration.

Unveil the Magic

As you dive into the rich chapters that await, allow your curiosity to unfold like a delicate blossom. Discover the hidden treasures of characters, the harmonies of tones, and the stories that resonate across cultures. Each day you spend with the Chitchat Chronicles will bring you closer to fluency, bridging gaps and fostering connections you might never have imagined.

Begin Your Odyssey

So, dear reader, with your aspirations as your compass and the Chitchat Chronicles as your map, let the journey commence. Delve into the pages ahead, let the stories enchant you, and the tones captivate your ear. As Mandarin Chinese unveils its secrets, may you find not just a new language but a profound appreciation for the symphony of humanity's shared voices.

Prepare to embark on an odyssey that traverses languages, cultures, and hearts. Welcome to the Chitchat Chronicles, where language is more than words – it's a bridge to understanding, a key to connection, and a tapestry woven with threads of wisdom and wonder.

Let the adventure begin.

CHAPTER 1

Beginnings of a Linguistic Voyage: Exploring Mandarin Through Stories and Mastering Accents

Embarking on a linguistic voyage is like setting sail into uncharted waters, where the destination holds the promise of new perspectives, cultural enrichment, and cognitive growth. This chapter introduces readers to a captivating journey of learning Mandarin, one of the most intricate and fascinating languages in the world. Through the art of storytelling and the mastery of accents, learners are invited to immerse themselves in the depths of Mandarin, unlocking not only linguistic proficiency but also a deeper understanding of Chinese culture and history.

The Intricacies of Mandarin: A Brief Overview

Mandarin, the most widely spoken language in the world, presents learners with a rich tapestry of tonal nuances, characters, and cultural connotations. Rooted in a history that spans millennia, Mandarin has evolved into a dynamic language that embodies the essence of China's social, political, and artistic evolution.

Exploring Tones: A Musical Journey

At the heart of Mandarin lies its tonal nature, where a single word's meaning can drastically change based on the tone with which it's spoken. Four fundamental tones, plus a neutral tone, challenge learners to attune their ears to a symphony of rising, falling, and fluctuating melodies. To aid learners in mastering these tones, the chapter explore deeply into interactive exercises and engaging audio resources, guiding them through a musical journey of pronunciation perfection.

Unveiling Characters: The Art of Visual Language

The Mandarin writing system, with its intricate characters derived from pictorial origins, provides a gateway into Chinese culture and philosophy. By weaving character analysis into the linguistic voyage, learners can decipher the historical context, radical components, and stroke order that shape each character's significance. Through a series of captivating stories, readers not only grasp the beauty of character composition but also deepen their connection to the language's cultural heritage.

Storytelling: An Immersive Learning Experience

Incorporating storytelling into Mandarin language acquisition enhances comprehension, memory retention, and cultural appreciation. The chapter introduces learners to a collection of captivating stories, each carefully crafted to weave language elements, idiomatic expressions, and historical references seamlessly.

Journey to the Silk Road: An Epic Adventure

One compelling narrative takes readers on a voyage along the ancient Silk Road, where they traverse bustling marketplaces, encounter diverse characters, and unravel the threads of trade and diplomacy that shaped China's history. Through vivid descriptions and dialogues, learners not only absorb essential vocabulary and grammar but also become absorbed in the cultural mosaic that influenced Mandarin's evolution.

Whispers of the Forbidden City: Love and Intrigue

Within the majestic walls of the Forbidden City, a tale of forbidden love and political intrigue unfolds, capturing readers' imagination while advancing their language skills. By introducing relatable characters facing timeless dilemmas, this story becomes a conduit for learning conversational Mandarin in context. Learners engage with idiomatic expressions, colloquial phrases, and everyday dialogue, thereby enhancing their ability to communicate effectively in real-life situations.

Mastering Accents: Bridging the Gap

Accent mastery serves as a bridge between linguistic comprehension and authentic communication. Mandarin, with its diverse range of regional accents, presents learners with the opportunity to embrace linguistic variation and connect with native speakers on a profound level.

From North to South: Exploring Regional Nuances

Through interactive exercises and guided practice, learners initiate a phonetic expedition, directing the distinct accents that flavor Mandarin across different regions of China. By dissecting phonetic elements and speech patterns unique to each area, readers not only enhance their listening skills but also cultivate an appreciation for the linguistic diversity that defines Mandarin's soundscape.

Embracing Authenticity: Conversational Fluency

The chapter empowers learners to move beyond textbook pronunciation and engage in authentic conversations with native speakers. By immersing themselves in recordings of real-life dialogues and practicing with language partners, readers gain the confidence to navigate the intricacies of spontaneous speech, respond with agility, and truly connect with Mandarin speakers around the world.

Cultural Context: Navigating Beyond Words

To master Mandarin is to venture beyond vocabulary and grammar into the intricate fabric of Chinese culture, history, and societal norms. The chapter provides readers with an insightful exploration of cultural nuances that empower them to communicate not just with words, but with a deep understanding of context.

The Art of Politeness: Etiquette and Expressions

Understanding the subtleties of politeness and respect is paramount when communicating in Mandarin. Readers are introduced to the intricate system of honorifics, gestures, and formal expressions that underpin Chinese social interactions. By embracing these cultural cues, learners navigate social situations with finesse and foster meaningful connections with native speakers.

Celebrating Festivals: Embracing Traditions

Incorporating Mandarin into cultural celebrations transforms language learning into a holistic experience. The chapter investigate thoroughly into major Chinese festivals, such as Lunar New Year and Mid-Autumn Festival, unraveling the stories, rituals, and idioms that characterize these occasions. Through this exploration, learners deepen their appreciation for Chinese customs and traditions, while acquiring the language skills to engage in authentic festive exchanges.

Setting Sail for Proficiency

As readers conclude this chapter, they have not only embarked on a linguistic voyage but have also uncovered the transformative power of Mandarin storytelling and accent mastery. The journey has taken them through the tonal symphony of Mandarin, guided them through captivating narratives that embody cultural richness, and equipped them with the tools to communicate authentically in diverse scenarios.

This chapter stands as an invitation to dive deeper into the ocean of Mandarin, where the horizon holds endless possibilities for exploration, connection, and personal growth. As learners continue their voyage, they carry with them the stories, accents, and cultural insights that make the Mandarin language not just a means of communication, but a vessel for experiencing the heart and soul of China.

In the words of Confucius, "A journey of a thousand miles begins with a single step." With this chapter as their guide, readers take that first step on a linguistic journey that promises to enrich their lives in ways they could have never imagined.

CHAPTER 2

Mastering the Melodies of Mandarin: Pitch Perfect - Navigating Tones and Pronunciation

Language is a symphony of sounds, where each note carries meaning and nuance. In the realm of Mandarin Chinese, this symphony takes on a unique form, defined by its tonal nature. Mastery of Mandarin pronunciation, particularly its intricate tonal system, is not only a linguistic endeavor but a journey into the heart of Chinese culture and communication. This essay examines closely into the art of mastering the melodies of Mandarin, exploring the significance of tones and pronunciation accuracy in achieving effective communication and cultural connection.

Tonal Marvels: Decoding Mandarin's Musical Language

Mandarin Chinese is often characterized by its four fundamental tones, plus a neutral tone. Each tone carries a distinct pitch contour that differentiates words from one another, rendering the same sequence of phonemes into entirely different meanings. The significance of tones in Mandarin cannot be understated; they are the building blocks of communication, infusing words with layers of interpretation and context.

The Four Tones: A Musical Journey

The first tone is a high, level pitch that remains constant, akin to singing a single note. The second tone rises from a mid-level pitch to a higher one, like asking a question in English. The third tone starts mid-level, dips down, and then rises again, resembling a falling then rising curve. The fourth tone is a sharp, downward pitch, akin to a command or an exclamation. The neutral tone, though less defined in pitch, adds complexity through its interactions with adjacent tones.

Pitch Perfect Pronunciation: The Key to Clarity

Accurate pronunciation of tones is essential for mutual comprehension, as mispronunciation can lead to confusion and unintended meanings. To master the art of Mandarin pronunciation, learners must attune their ears to the distinct melodies of each tone and practice producing them with precision. Interactive exercises, audio resources, and guidance from native speakers contribute to the refinement of pronunciation skills, ensuring that each word resonates with its intended meaning.

Cultural Significance: Tones as Cultural Markers

Tones in Mandarin are not merely linguistic elements; they are cultural markers that reveal much about societal values, historical contexts, and interpersonal dynamics. Properly employing tones demonstrates respect for the language and the culture it represents, enhancing cross-cultural interactions and deepening connections with native speakers.

The Subtle Art of Politeness

In Mandarin, the choice of tone can communicate politeness and formality. Addressing someone using the appropriate tone conveys respect and consideration, crucial in maintaining harmonious social interactions. The usage of honorifics, along with correct tone placement, reflects the intricate dance of etiquette and hierarchy woven into Chinese society.

The Expressive Canvas of Emotions

Tones in Mandarin also facilitate emotional expression. A shift in tone can transform a statement into a question, inject enthusiasm or urgency, and convey emotions ranging from excitement to frustration. By mastering the art of tonal modulation, learners unlock the ability to convey a spectrum of feelings, infusing their language with authenticity and depth.

Pitching for Proficiency: Navigating Challenges

While mastering Mandarin tones is a rewarding pursuit, it comes with its fair share of challenges. Learners from non-tonal language backgrounds may initially struggle to distinguish between tones or replicate them accurately. However, with perseverance and targeted practice, these challenges can be overcome, leading to heightened fluency and a deeper connection with Mandarin-speaking communities.

The Intonation Conundrum

One challenge arises from the concept of intonation in tonal languages. Intonation, which refers to the rise and fall of the voice within a sentence, can vary across languages. For non-tonal language speakers, adapting to Mandarin's intonation patterns while maintaining correct tones can be perplexing. However, through attentive listening and mimicking native speakers, learners gradually internalize these patterns, transforming intonation into an asset rather than a hindrance.

The Perils of Tonal Confusion

Another hurdle is the potential for tonal confusion, wherein similar-sounding words with different tones can lead to miscommunication. This challenge emphasizes the importance of context in Mandarin communication. Contextual cues, such as surrounding words and sentence structure, aid in clarifying the intended meaning, demonstrating that while tones are pivotal, they are part of a broader communication framework.

Unlocking Melodic Mastery: Strategies for Success

The journey towards mastering the melodies of Mandarin requires a multifaceted approach that combines theoretical understanding, attentive practice, and cultural immersion.

Several strategies can guide learners toward achieving pitch-perfect pronunciation and seamless tonal integration.

Auditory Training: Tuning the Ear

A fundamental step in mastering tones is developing acute auditory discernment. Learners can engage with audio materials, such as podcasts, songs, and dialogues, to familiarize themselves with the tonal nuances of Mandarin. Regular exposure to native speakers' speech patterns hones the ear's ability to detect subtle pitch changes and enhances overall listening comprehension.

Replication and Reflection

Mirroring native speakers' pronunciation is a powerful technique for tone acquisition. Replicating speech patterns and recording one's own voice aids in identifying areas of improvement. Self-assessment, along with feedback from language partners or instructors, accelerates progress by pinpointing areas requiring attention.

Contextual Practice: The Role of Sentences

Tone accuracy within sentences is equally crucial. By practicing tones in context, learners grasp the flow of natural speech and refine their ability to maintain tonal consistency. This approach also highlights the relationship between tones and sentence stress, further enriching the melodic quality of spoken Mandarin

Harmonizing Fluency and Culture

Mastering the melodies of Mandarin transcends linguistic proficiency; it is an endeavor that intertwines language, culture, and human connection. The nuances of tones and pronunciation breathe life into Mandarin, allowing learners to communicate not only with words but also with emotions, intentions, and cultural awareness. By piloting the intricate world of tones, learners not only unlock effective communication but also forge a deeper bond with the language and its people.

In the grand symphony of language, Mandarin's tonal melodies offer a gateway to understanding and experiencing the rich tapestry of Chinese culture. Just as a musician refines their technique to play a piece of music flawlessly, learners of Mandarin strive for pitch-perfect pronunciation to communicate with clarity, authenticity, and resonance. With dedication, practice, and a discerning ear, mastering the melodies of Mandarin becomes a journey of discovery, where each tone resonates with the beauty of language and the depth of human expression.

Beyond Fluency: Tones as Cultural Bridges

The journey to mastering Mandarin's tones goes beyond the realm of language acquisition; it forges connections that transcend words. Tones are cultural bridges that enable learners to immerse themselves in the heart of Chinese society, enhancing cross-cultural understanding and facilitating authentic interactions.

Empathy through Tonal Sensitivity

Tonal sensitivity fosters empathy and respect for the nuances embedded within Mandarin. By appreciating the cultural significance of tones, learners not only avoid misunderstandings but also exhibit a willingness to engage with Mandarin on a deeper level. This sensitivity extends to Chinese speakers, demonstrating a genuine desire to communicate effectively and to honor the intricacies of their language.

The Subtleties of Humor and Wit

Mandarin tones lend themselves to humor and wordplay, often capitalizing on the potential for tonal confusion to create clever puns or witty expressions. A deep understanding of tones allows learners to appreciate and even participate in such linguistic play, fostering a sense of camaraderie and shared humor with native speakers. This cultural insight enriches interpersonal relationships and enhances language enjoyment.

Tonal Mastery as a Gateway to Proficiency

Tonal mastery is a foundational pillar of language proficiency, setting the stage for broader linguistic achievements. Once learners navigate the complexities of Mandarin's melodies, they are better equipped to tackle other linguistic facets, such as grammar, vocabulary expansion, and advanced language structures.

Grammatical Intuition: Tones as Punctuation

Tones play a subtle role in indicating grammatical structures, serving as a form of punctuation within spoken Mandarin. The rising second tone, for instance, often marks questions, while the fourth tone signifies the completion of an action. Recognizing these tonal cues aids in deciphering sentence structures and inferring grammatical meaning, leading to a more intuitive grasp of the language's syntax.

Vocabulary Expansion: Tone Patterns

The mastery of tones can also facilitate vocabulary acquisition. By recognizing recurring tone patterns, learners can predict the tones of unfamiliar words, thereby expanding their vocabulary with greater ease. This predictive ability minimizes the need for rote memorization and allows learners to deduce tones based on familiarity with similar word structures.

Navigating Dialectal Diversity: Tones in Regional Variation

Mandarin's tonal melodies traverse not only linguistic diversity but also regional variation. While the standard tone system serves as a unifying force, different dialects and accents within Mandarin introduce variations that enrich the language's melodic tapestry.

Embracing Regional Nuance

Regional variations in tones reflect the cultural and historical diversity of Mandarin-speaking communities. For example, the Beijing dialect, upon which Standard Mandarin is largely based, may differ in tones from southern dialects like Cantonese. By embracing these nuances, learners gain insight into the cultural mosaic of Mandarin-speaking regions, enabling them to connect with a wider array of speakers.

A Harmonious Symphony of Language and Culture

In the intricate world of Mandarin, tones and pronunciation are more than linguistic components; they are the threads that weave together the fabric of language and culture. Mastery of these tonal melodies unlocks the doors to effective communication, cultural appreciation, and the forging of meaningful connections with Mandarin speakers around the world.

Just as a musical composition is enriched by the precise interplay of notes, the mastery of Mandarin's tones enhances communication, allowing learners to convey not only words but also emotions, intentions, and cultural nuances. As learners navigate the complexities of pitch and melody, they Start an adventure in a journey that resonates with the harmonies of language and the symphony of human expression.

In the realm of Mandarin, fluency is not just about speaking; it's about singing the melodic narratives of a culture, capturing its essence through the rise and fall of tones. As learners continue to refine their pronunciation, they engage in a lifelong partnership with the language, where each tone struck is a note in the grand symphony of communication. Ultimately, mastering the melodies of Mandarin transcends the boundaries of language, echoing the universal truth that the beauty of human connection is harmonized through the cadence of understanding.

CHAPTER 3

Pinyin Playground: Unveiling Pinyin - Your Bridge to Mandarin Pronunciation

Welcome back to the captivating world of the Pinyin Playground! Throughout this chapter, we scrutinize deeper into the heart of Mandarin pronunciation by exploring the essential role of Pinyin in bridging the gap between language learners and the rich tapestry of Mandarin sounds. As we navigate through the Pinyin Playground, you'll uncover how Pinyin serves as your invaluable guide, helping you decode the melodies of Mandarin and empowering you to engage confidently in everyday scenarios. Set yourself for the task to start an adventure that unveils the power of Pinyin as your gateway to effective communication and cultural connection.

The Pinyin-Mandarin Connection: Navigating Everyday Scenarios

1. Greetings and Introductions: Picture yourself confidently strolling through the bustling streets of a Chinese city. Armed with Pinyin, you'll effortlessly exchange greetings and introduce yourself to locals. Mastering Pinyin's sounds enables you to pronounce common greetings like **"你好" (nǐ hǎo) - "hello"** - with finesse, instantly creating a positive impression and connecting with Mandarin speakers on a personal level.

2. Ordering Food Adventures: Imagine stepping into a local eatery and effortlessly placing your order using Pinyin. Pinyin ensures that you can confidently request favorites like **"炸鸡" (zhá jī) - "fried chicken"** - without the fear of mispronunciation. By employing Pinyin accurately, you not only satisfy your culinary cravings but also immerse yourself in the flavors of Chinese cuisine, bonding with locals over shared culinary experiences.

3. Asking for Directions: Navigating a new city becomes a breeze with Pinyin as your compass. As you inquire about directions using phrases like **"请问"** (**qǐng wèn**) - **"excuse me"** - followed by clear Pinyin pronunciation, you navigate through the urban landscape with confidence and poise. Pinyin transforms you from a lost wanderer into an empowered explorer, seamlessly interacting with locals and unveiling the beauty of new surroundings.

Pinyin and Characters: Your Dual Roadmap

1. Mapping Pinyin to Characters: In the Pinyin Playground, you not only learn Pinyin sounds but also uncover its crucial role as a roadmap to understanding Chinese characters. By pairing Pinyin with characters, you unlock the door to reading and writing, making the seemingly daunting task of character learning more manageable and enjoyable. As you encounter Pinyin in your language learning journey, you're simultaneously building the foundation for a lifelong relationship with Mandarin characters.

2. Pinyin's Phonetic Clues: Pinyin acts as a powerful mnemonic device, aiding memory retention and character recognition. Each Pinyin sound provides a phonetic clue to

the pronunciation of its corresponding character. For instance, the Pinyin **"bù"** matches the character **"不,"** both sharing the same initial consonant sound, which reinforces the connection between sound and symbol, propelling your character-learning progress.

Cultural Connections through Pinyin

1. Bridging Cultural Barriers: Pinyin serves as a cultural bridge, enabling you to communicate beyond words. Through accurate pronunciation, you demonstrate respect for the language and its cultural nuances. This gesture of cultural appreciation fosters connections and elicits warmth from native speakers, transforming language interactions into meaningful cultural exchanges.

2. Cultural Nuances in Pinyin: Probe deeper into cultural subtleties by exploring Pinyin's role in expressing politeness and formality. For instance, the phrase **"谢谢" (xiè xiè)** -

"thank you" - can be elevated to a more formal tone by enunciating each syllable distinctly. By mastering these nuances, you enrich your language interactions, building bridges of cultural understanding and demonstrating your commitment to effective communication.

Pinyin: Your Versatile Companion

1. Pinyin's Portability: Pinyin becomes your trusty companion, accessible anywhere and everywhere. Whether you're reading signs, menus, or text messages, Pinyin offers instant guidance, ensuring that you can decipher the Mandarin sounds with ease. Its versatility transforms every moment into an opportunity for learning and connection, reinforcing your commitment to mastering Mandarin pronunciation.

2. Pinyin's Lifelong Utility: Your journey through the Pinyin Playground is not just a temporary adventure; it equips you with a lifelong skill. The proficiency you gain in Pinyin transcends language barriers and remains relevant as you progress in your Mandarin studies. Whether you're engaging in casual conversations, giving presentations, or traveling, Pinyin continues to serve as your compass, guiding you toward clear and confident communication.

Embrace the Power of Pinyin

As we conclude our exploration of the Pinyin Playground, you've unraveled the transformative power of Pinyin as your bridge to Mandarin pronunciation. Through Pinyin, you've acquired a tool that empowers you to engage with locals, navigate cultural nuances, and create lasting connections. With each accurate pronunciation, you're not only mastering sounds; you're unlocking doors to immersive cultural experiences and meaningful language interactions.

Just as a bridge connects two shores, Pinyin bridges the gap between you and the vibrant world of Mandarin sounds. Embrace Pinyin as your steadfast guide, and let its melodies guide you toward a journey of linguistic mastery, cultural appreciation, and unforgettable experiences. The Pinyin Playground is your gateway to the symphony of Mandarin, and your adventure has only just begun.

Embracing Pinyin as Your Partner in Progress

As you journey deeper into the world of Mandarin pronunciation, it's important to embrace Pinyin as your partner in progress. Here are some additional insights and tips to ensure your mastery of Pinyin becomes an integral part of your language learning voyage:

1. Practice Makes Perfect: Like any skill, mastering Pinyin requires consistent practice. Incorporate daily Pinyin practice sessions into your language learning routine. Utilize

online resources, mobile apps, and language exchange partners to fine-tune your pronunciation and ensure accuracy.

2. Listen and Repeat: Engaging your auditory senses is crucial for Pinyin mastery. Listen to native speakers, watch movies or TV shows in Mandarin, and mimic their pronunciation. Repetition helps your brain internalize the correct sounds and tones.

3. Slow and Steady Wins: While enthusiasm is key, remember that learning Mandarin pronunciation is a gradual process. Start with mastering the basics before progressing to more complex sounds and tone combinations. Patience and persistence will yield the best results.

4. Record and Review: Record yourself speaking Mandarin using Pinyin and listen for areas of improvement. Compare your recordings to native speakers to identify gaps in pronunciation. Regular self-assessment and reflection are powerful tools for growth.

5. Use Pinyin for Vocabulary Building: Pinyin isn't just for pronunciation; it's a fantastic tool for expanding your vocabulary. As you encounter new words and characters, pay

attention to their Pinyin representations. This aids in memory retention and reinforces correct pronunciation.

6. Immerse Yourself: Create an immersive environment by surrounding yourself with Pinyin. Label objects in your living space with their Pinyin names, write notes or journal entries using Pinyin, and incorporate Pinyin into your language learning games.

7. Language Exchange and Conversation: Engage in language exchange sessions or conversational practice with native speakers. Pinyin serves as a valuable tool for communicating effectively, even as you work towards more advanced language proficiency.

Beyond Pinyin: Your Path to Fluency

While mastering Pinyin is a vital step in your Mandarin language journey, it's important to recognize that Pinyin is just one piece of the puzzle. As you continue to refine your pronunciation, remember that Pinyin is a stepping stone to achieving broader language goals:

1. Character Learning: Building on your Pinyin foundation, investigate thoroughly into character learning. With Pinyin

as your guide, you'll find it easier to associate sounds with characters, facilitating the reading and writing process.

2. Tonal Acumen: Your proficiency in Pinyin tones will prove invaluable as you encounter more complex tone combinations and variations. Accurate tone usage is fundamental for clear communication and meaningful expression.

3. Grammar and Structure: Mastering Pinyin pronunciation contributes to the overall fluidity of your spoken Mandarin. As you progress, focus on incorporating correct grammar, sentence structures, and idiomatic expressions to enhance your language fluency.

Your Pinyin-Pronunciation Success Story

Congratulations! You've traversed the Pinyin Playground and uncovered the profound role that Pinyin plays in shaping your Mandarin pronunciation skills. Through accurate Pinyin usage, you've embarked on a journey that transcends sounds; you've opened doors to cultural connections, confident communication, and immersive language experiences.

As you continue to refine your Pinyin pronunciation and progress in your Mandarin studies, remember that Pinyin is your steadfast companion. Its guidance and insights will accompany you on every step of your language learning voyage, ensuring that you navigate the complexities of Mandarin pronunciation with finesse and authenticity.

Embrace Pinyin not only as a tool but as a gateway to a world of linguistic and cultural exploration. With Pinyin by your side, you're not just learning sounds; you're embarking on a remarkable journey of understanding, connection, and self-discovery through the beauty of Mandarin pronunciation.

Chapter 4

Conversational Cornerstones: Greetings Galore - Initiating Conversations with Confidence

Welcome to the vibrant world of Conversational Cornerstones! In this section, we will explore the essential art of greetings and introductions, to equip you with the tools to initiate conversations with confidence and authenticity. Greetings serve as the gateway to meaningful interactions, allowing you to forge connections, bridge cultural gaps, and navigate social situations with ease. As we explore the diverse array of greetings in Mandarin, you'll unlock the key to unlocking the hearts and minds of native speakers, fostering relationships that extend beyond language. Prepare to take action to set out upon a course to a journey that unveils the magic of greetings and sets the stage for engaging conversations.

The Significance of Greetings: Beyond Words

1. A Cultural Prelude: Greetings in Mandarin encompass more than just words; they encapsulate cultural values and norms. Understanding and using greetings correctly demonstrates respect for the culture and a genuine interest in meaningful communication. By embracing greetings, you're not just speaking; you're extending a hand of friendship and cultural appreciation.

2. Building Bridges: Greetings serve as bridges between individuals from different backgrounds. A well-delivered greeting instantly breaks down barriers, creating a welcoming atmosphere and fostering an environment of openness. Greetings are the catalyst for connection, enabling you to relate to others on a personal level, regardless of linguistic differences.

Greetings Galore: Unveiling Mandarin's Diverse Greeting Repertoire

1. The Classic **"你好"** (nǐ hǎo) - **"Hello"**: Dive into the cornerstone of Mandarin greetings. Master the correct pronunciation of **"你好"** and discover its versatility in various contexts. Whether you're meeting someone for the first time or reuniting with a friend, **"你好"** is your go-to phrase for extending warm regards.

2. **"早上好"** (zǎo shàng hǎo) - **"Good Morning"**: Embrace the charm of starting your day with a friendly **"早上好."** Explore the nuances of morning greetings and experience how this phrase connects you to the rhythm of daily life in Mandarin-speaking regions.

3. **"晚上好"** (wǎn shàng hǎo) - **"Good Evening"**: Transition seamlessly from day to night with the graceful **"晚上好."** Uncover the cultural context of evening greetings and learn to use this phrase to create an atmosphere of warmth and cordiality.

4. **"你吃了吗？"** (nǐ chī le ma?) - **"Have You Eaten?"**: Discover the cultural depth embedded in this seemingly simple greeting. Explore its origins and understand how it reflects hospitality, care, and concern for others' well-being.

5. **"见面好" (jiàn miàn hǎo) - "Nice to Meet You":** Unveil the excitement of meeting new people with the delightful phrase **"见面好."** Grasp the nuances of this expression and experience how it paves the way for delightful conversations and new connections.

Navigating Social Contexts: Greetings for Every Occasion

1. Formal and Informal Scenarios: Explore the art of tailoring your greetings to different social contexts. Learn when to employ formal expressions, such as **"您好" (nín hǎo),** and when to opt for a more casual tone, like **"嗨" (hāi),** as you engage in diverse interactions.

2. Workplace Dynamics: Scrutinize the intricacies of greetings within professional settings. Discover how phrases like **"工作顺利" (gōng zuò shùn lì) - "May your work go smoothly"** - foster positive relationships and create a harmonious work environment.

Cultural Nuances and Gestures

1. The Power of Nonverbal Communication: Understand the significance of nonverbal cues, such as bowing, nodding, and smiling, to enhance the impact of your greetings. Discover how these gestures align with Mandarin greetings and facilitate effective cross-cultural communication.

2. Pronunciation and Accent: Embrace the role of accurate pronunciation and accent in greetings. Fine-tune your tones and sounds to ensure your greetings are not only understood but also convey genuine respect and appreciation.

Greetings in Action: Real-Life Scenarios

1. Marketplace Conversations: Begin a virtual journey through a bustling market, where greetings open the doors to vibrant interactions with local vendors. Experience the joy of connecting with traders and learn to use greetings as a means of building rapport and gaining insights into local culture.

2. Café Culture: Immerse yourself in the ambiance of a cozy café and observe how greetings enhance your experience. Engage in coffee shop conversations, practicing your greetings as you order your favorite beverage and strike up conversations with fellow patrons.

3. Navigating Public Transportation: As you navigate the public transportation landscape, master the art of greetings in travel-related scenarios. From asking for directions to striking up conversations with fellow passengers, you'll harness the power of greetings to ease your journey and foster connections.

Mastering the Art of Effective Greetings

To truly harness the power of greetings and initiate conversations with confidence, here are some practical tips and insights to enhance your mastery:

1. Cultural Sensitivity: Recognize the cultural nuances associated with greetings. Different cultures may have varying levels of formality, gestures, and expressions. Demonstrating cultural sensitivity in your greetings showcases your respect for local customs and fosters genuine connections.

2. Learn from Native Speakers: Engage with native speakers to observe and imitate their greetings. Listening to authentic conversations allows you to capture intonation, rhythm, and natural expressions, enhancing your ability to deliver greetings naturally.

3. Practice Role Play: Engage in role-play scenarios to simulate real-life interactions. Whether you're greeting a colleague, a friend, or a stranger, practicing different situations enhances your adaptability and confidence in using greetings appropriately.

4. Expand Your Repertoire: While the chapter introduces key greetings, explore additional phrases to diversify your conversational toolbox. Phrases like **"好久不见" (hǎo jiǔ bù jiàn) - "Long time no see" - or "请多关照" (qǐng duō guān zhào) - "Please take care of me"** - add depth to your interactions.

5. Genuine Expression: Infuse your greetings with authenticity. A sincere smile, eye contact, and a warm tone convey genuine interest and openness, transcending language barriers and fostering meaningful connections.

Bridging Language and Culture

1. Language Exchange Partners: Engage in language exchange partnerships to practice greetings with native speakers. This immersive experience allows you to receive

immediate feedback and gain cultural insights that enrich your language journey.

2. Cultural Workshops: Attend cultural workshops or events to deepen your understanding of greetings in specific contexts. These experiences provide hands-on learning and immerse you in authentic cultural practices.

3. Travel and Cultural Immersion: Kickstart a journey to travel adventures to Mandarin-speaking regions. Interacting with locals in their natural environment exposes you to a multitude of greetings and allows you to embrace the heart of the culture firsthand.

Expanding Conversational Horizons

As you master the art of greetings and initiate conversations with confidence, remember that greetings are just the beginning. They open the door to deeper dialogues, shared experiences, and genuine connections. Here are some pathways to expand your conversational horizons:

1. Personal Introductions: Following greetings, introduce yourself and share a few basic details about your background, interests, and purpose. This encourages a

reciprocal exchange of information and sets the stage for meaningful conversations.

2. Asking Open-Ended Questions: Transition from greetings to open-ended questions that invite conversation. Inquire about someone's day, interests, or experiences, demonstrating your genuine curiosity and eagerness to engage.

3. Active Listening: Engage in active listening to show interest in your conversation partner's responses. Respond thoughtfully, building upon their comments and fostering a dynamic exchange of ideas.

4. Sharing Experiences: Draw from your own experiences to contribute to the conversation. Sharing anecdotes, observations, or opinions enriches the dialogue and creates a sense of camaraderie.

5. Language Exchange: Engage in language exchange partnerships or group conversations to practice greetings and engage in varied discussions. These interactions expose you to different speaking styles and offer opportunities to expand your vocabulary.

The Legacy of Greetings

As we conclude our exploration of Greetings Galore, you've journeyed through the heart of conversational interactions, discovering how greetings serve as the foundation of authentic connections. In every **"你好" (nǐ hǎo) and "早上好" (zǎo shàng hǎo),** you've encountered the magic of bridging cultures, fostering relationships, and igniting conversations that transcend language barriers.

During your continuous language learning voyage, embrace the legacy of greetings as a beacon of light that guides you through the intricacies of human interaction. Just as a warm handshake or a friendly smile transcends words, your mastery of greetings unveils a world of understanding, empathy, and shared experiences. Through greetings, you've unlocked the door to meaningful conversations that weave the fabric of cross-cultural understanding, leaving an indelible mark on your journey of language mastery and cultural immersion.

CHAPTER 5

Café Chronicles: Sips and Sentences - Ordering at Cafés in Mandarin

Welcome to the delightful realm of Café Chronicles! In this chapter, we set off on a journey through the cozy ambiance of cafés, where the aroma of freshly brewed coffee and the allure of delectable pastries envelop us. As you step into cafés in Mandarin-speaking regions, the ability to order your favorite beverages and treats becomes a doorway to cultural immersion and authentic experiences. Through this chapter, you'll master the art of ordering at cafés in Mandarin, navigating menus with confidence, and engaging in delightful exchanges with café staff. Ready up your tools to indulge in the rich flavors of language and culture as we dive into the world of Café Chronicles.

The Café Experience: Beyond Beverages

1. Café Culture and Language: Cafés are not merely places to grab a drink; they are cultural hubs where people gather, relax, and converse. Mastering the language of cafés allows you to participate in this cherished cultural experience, connecting with locals and fellow patrons over shared moments of leisure.

2. Language as a Gateway: Ordering at cafés serves as a gateway to more profound cultural encounters. By navigating menus, conversing with staff, and interacting with fellow café-goers, you open doors to meaningful connections and authentic insights into daily life.

Sips and Sentences: Decoding Café Menus

1. Navigating the Menu: Step by step, we'll decode the intricacies of café menus in Mandarin. From identifying different types of beverages to understanding ingredient descriptions, you'll build the confidence to explore menus and make selections that suit your taste.

2. Ordering Like a Pro: Discover essential sentence structures and vocabulary to place your orders with finesse. Whether you're craving a cappuccino, a green tea latte, or a

savory pastry, you'll learn how to articulate your preferences and customize your orders.

3. Special Requests and Allergies: Investigate deeply into the art of conveying special requests and dietary restrictions. Master the language to communicate allergies, substitutions, or modifications, ensuring a seamless and enjoyable café experience tailored to your needs.

The Art of Conversation: Engaging with Café Staff

1. Initiating Conversation: Beyond ordering, engage in pleasant exchanges with café staff. Master the art of polite greetings and inquire about recommendations, creating a friendly atmosphere that enhances your café interactions.

2. Expressing Gratitude: Learn to express gratitude and appreciation for the service provided. Discover phrases that convey your satisfaction and leave a positive impression, fostering a harmonious rapport with café staff.

Café Chronicles in Action: Real-Life Scenarios

1. Morning Brew: Step into a café on a bustling morning, where you'll practice ordering your preferred morning beverage with confidence. Experience the joy of engaging

with café staff and fellow patrons, setting the tone for a delightful day.

2. Afternoon Indulgence: Set sail on an afternoon adventure, where you'll master the language to order a variety of beverages and treats. Engage in conversations with staff and immerse yourself in the ambiance of the café, savoring the flavors of language and culture.

3. Sharing Moments: Explore the art of ordering for a group of friends or colleagues. Navigate the menu, customize orders, and engage in friendly interactions, showcasing your ability to navigate social situations and create enjoyable café moments.

Café Etiquette and Cultural Nuances

1. Seating and Behavior: Unveil the unwritten rules of café etiquette. Learn about appropriate seating, tipping practices, and how to conduct yourself in a way that aligns with local customs, creating a seamless café experience.

2. Small Talk and Connections: Embrace the role of small talk in café conversations. Discover how casual conversations with café staff and fellow patrons can lead to meaningful connections and enriching cultural insights.

Beyond Cafés: Language for Everyday Use

1. Language Transferability: Recognize the transferability of café language to other social settings. The skills you acquire while ordering at cafés, such as sentence construction and communication techniques, extend to diverse scenarios, enhancing your overall language proficiency.

2. Personal Empowerment: As you master the art of ordering at cafés, you empower yourself to navigate similar interactions in different contexts. Whether you're in a restaurant, a market, or a public transport station, your café language skills become a versatile tool for effective communication.

Refining Your Café Language Mastery

To enhance your proficiency in ordering at cafés in Mandarin, consider these practical tips and strategies:

1. Menu Exploration: Familiarize yourself with common café vocabulary by exploring menus online or in local cafés. Take note of beverage names, ingredient descriptions, and special offerings to expand your repertoire of ordering phrases.

2. Language Apps: Utilize language learning apps to practice café-related vocabulary and sentence structures. Many apps offer interactive lessons and quizzes that simulate real café scenarios, allowing you to refine your skills in a dynamic and engaging manner.

3. Language Partners: Engage in language exchange partnerships or conversation practice sessions with native speakers. Role-play café interactions to gain firsthand experience and receive feedback on your pronunciation and delivery.

4. Café Visits: Embrace authentic experiences by visiting cafés in Mandarin-speaking regions. Immerse yourself in the ambiance, observe how locals interact, and practice ordering with confidence. Each café visit becomes an opportunity to refine your skills and enjoy cultural immersion.

5. Review and Repetition: Regularly review café-related vocabulary and phrases to reinforce your memory. Repetition is key to solidifying your language skills and ensuring that you can confidently order beverages and engage in conversations.

Café Conversations: Expanding Horizons

As you are managing your way through the world of café interactions, remember that the skills you acquire extend beyond ordering beverages. Embrace the art of conversation to broaden your language proficiency and cultural engagement:

1. Engaging in Small Talk: Beyond placing orders, engage in casual conversations with café staff and fellow patrons. Inquire about the café's specialties, share your preferences, and exchange pleasantries to create a friendly and welcoming atmosphere.

2. Cultural Exchanges: Capitalize on café interactions to learn more about local culture and customs. Ask about the origins of certain beverages, learn about café traditions, and gather insights from locals to deepen your cultural understanding.

3. Café Stories: Share anecdotes and stories during your café visits. Whether it's a travel adventure, a memorable experience, or a personal reflection, weaving narratives into your conversations fosters connection and encourages meaningful exchanges.

Language Transfer and Versatility

Recognize the transferability of your café language skills to various social contexts:

1. Restaurant Experiences: Your proficiency in ordering at cafés lays the foundation for ordering in restaurants and eateries. Apply similar sentence structures and vocabulary to navigate menus and engage with waitstaff effectively.

2. Marketplace Interactions: Transfer your skills to interactions at local markets and food stalls. The ability to communicate preferences, make inquiries, and engage in conversations serves you well as you explore culinary offerings.

3. Public Transport Communication: Extend your café language proficiency to public transport settings. Communicate with ticket sellers, inquire about routes, and navigate transportation options using similar communication techniques.

Café Chronicles: A Taste of Language Mastery

In the tapestry of language learning, Café Chronicles stand as a testament to your commitment, enthusiasm, and adaptability. By mastering the art of ordering at cafés in Mandarin, you've embraced language as a conduit for cultural experiences, a tool for connection, and a pathway to genuine interactions. Your ability to engage confidently in café conversations reflects the heart of language learning: the pursuit of understanding, empathy, and shared moments of joy.

In the trajectory of your language journey, remember that Café Chronicles symbolize more than just ordering beverages. They epitomize your readiness to explore, connect, and engage with the world around you. Each cup of coffee, every pastry enjoyed, and every sentence uttered becomes a step toward linguistic fluency and cross-cultural enrichment. Embrace the journey of Café Chronicles, savoring language and culture, one sip and sentence at a time.

CHAPTER 6

Market Mingle: Market Magic - Conversations and Bargains Made Easy

Step into the lively world of Market Mingle, where the bustling ambiance of local markets comes to life through conversations and bargains. Within this chapter, we will investigate deeply the vibrant tapestry of market experiences, equipping you with the language and skills to navigate markets in Mandarin-speaking regions with confidence and finesse. Markets are more than just places to shop; they are cultural hubs where interactions unfold, relationships are forged, and stories are shared. As we explore the art of market conversations and bargaining, you'll start a learning-oriented journey that empowers you to immerse yourself in local culture, connect with vendors, and negotiate with ease. Set yourself in motion to unveil the enchantment of Market Magic and embrace the thrill of successful market interactions.

The Essence of Market Mingle: Beyond Transactions

1. Cultural Insights Through Markets: Markets offer a unique window into the heart of a culture. By becoming involved in conversations and bargaining at markets, you gain insights into local customs, traditions, and ways of life, fostering a deeper connection to the community you're exploring.

2. Learning Through Interactions: Market Mingle is not only about shopping; it's an immersive learning opportunity. By engaging with vendors and fellow shoppers, you enhance your language skills, gain confidence in real-life interactions, and enrich your vocabulary with market-specific terms.

Market Conversations: Building Bridges Through Words

1. Greetings and Pleasantries: Master the art of initiating conversations with vendors through warm greetings and pleasantries. **"您好" (nín hǎo) - "Hello"** - becomes your

opening salutation, setting the tone for friendly and respectful interactions.

2. Inquiring About Goods: Discover effective ways to inquire about products. Learn questions like **"这个多少钱？"** **(zhè ge duō shǎo qián?)** - **"How much is this?"** - and **"你有没有…？"** **(nǐ yǒu méi yǒu?)** - **"Do you have…?"** - to express your interests and gather information about items for sale.

3. Descriptions and Preferences: Enhance your language proficiency by describing your preferences and seeking recommendations. Master phrases like **"我喜欢"** **(wǒ xǐ huān)** - **"I like"** - and **"有没有更大/更小的？"** **(yǒu méi yǒu gèng dà/gèng xiǎo de?)** - **"Do you have a bigger/smaller one?"** - to tailor your shopping experience.

Bargaining Brilliance: Navigating Price Negotiations

1. The Art of Bargaining: Explore the nuances of price negotiation in markets. Learn how to express your budget, counter offers, and engage in friendly bargaining while maintaining cultural sensitivity and respect.

2. Polite Persistence: Hone your bargaining skills through polite persistence. Utilize phrases like **"能便宜点吗？"** **(néng pián yi diǎn ma?) - "Can you make it cheaper?"** - to negotiate while preserving a harmonious and amicable atmosphere.

Market Mingle in Action: Real-Life Scenarios

1. Exploring Food Markets: Immerse yourself in a bustling food market, where you'll engage in conversations with local vendors to inquire about culinary delights. Sample street food, seek recommendations, and practice bargaining to curate your gastronomic adventure.

2. Artisanal Treasures: Undertake a journey through artisanal markets, where you'll converse with craftspeople and discover handmade treasures. Navigate discussions about craftsmanship, materials, and artistic techniques while building connections with creators.

3. Souvenirs and Keepsakes: Engage in market conversations to select souvenirs and keepsakes that capture the essence of your travels. Master vocabulary related to

local culture, landmarks, and symbols to curate meaningful mementos.

Cultural Etiquette and Empathy

1. Cultural Observations: Embrace cultural sensitivity by observing market practices and social dynamics. Recognize the importance of observing local customs, addressing vendors with respect, and adopting appropriate body language.

2. Understanding Market Rhythms: Familiarize yourself with market rhythms and peak times. Engaging with vendors during less busy periods may lead to more personalized interactions and a greater willingness to engage in conversation.

Learning Beyond Markets: Transferable Skills

1. Negotiation Skills: Recognize that the art of bargaining extends beyond markets. The negotiation skills you develop through market interactions can be applied to various scenarios, such as business negotiations and interpersonal communication.

2. Language Adaptability: Embrace the adaptability of the language skills you acquire in markets. The ability to initiate conversations, inquire about goods, and negotiate prices serves you well in diverse social settings.

The Magic of Market Mingle

As we conclude our exploration of Market Mingle, you've unlocked the enchanting realm where language, culture, and commerce converge. Through conversations and bargains, you've cultivated a deeper appreciation for the intricate threads that weave together the fabric of daily life in Mandarin-speaking regions. Each exchange and negotiation at the market has been a step toward linguistic empowerment and cultural connection.

Just as markets pulsate with energy and vibrancy, your Market Mingle experiences infuse your language journey with vitality and authenticity. Your ability to engage with vendors, navigate prices, and forge connections transforms markets into classrooms of cultural understanding and linguistic growth. Over the course of your journey, remember that the magic of Market Mingle lies not only in the items you acquire but, in the skills, memories, and insights you gather along the way.

Sustaining Your Market Mastery

To further refine your skills and continue embracing the magic of Market Mingle, consider these practical strategies:

1. Local Vocabulary: Familiarize yourself with market-specific vocabulary. Research common terms for various products and inquire about their names in Mandarin-speaking regions. This knowledge enhances your ability to engage in meaningful conversations with vendors.

2. Cultural Etiquette Research: Before visiting local markets, research cultural norms and etiquette specific to bargaining and interactions. Understanding the acceptable practices in each region fosters respectful and smooth interactions.

3. Language Apps and Resources: Utilize language apps and resources designed for market interactions. These tools often offer role-play scenarios, vocabulary lists, and audio samples that allow you to practice and improve your conversational skills.

4. Market Tours and Workshops: Participate in guided market tours or workshops offered in Mandarin-speaking areas. These experiences provide valuable insights, expose you to local interactions, and offer opportunities to practice conversations in authentic settings.

5. Feedback and Reflection: Seek feedback from native speakers or language exchange partners on your market conversations. Reflect on your experiences, identify areas for improvement, and celebrate your successes in engaging with vendors.

Expanding Conversational Horizons

1. Local Encounters: Extend your market language proficiency to daily encounters beyond the marketplace. Engage in conversations with locals at parks, public transportation, and community events to continue building connections.

2. Social Gatherings: Apply your bargaining skills in social settings where negotiation is involved, such as garage sales, flea markets, or charity events. Your ability to negotiate effectively enhances your interactions and contributes to successful outcomes.

3. Business and Professional Settings: Transfer your bargaining and conversation skills to business interactions. Negotiate contracts, agreements, and deals using the techniques and strategies you've honed in markets.

Market Mingle: A Journey of Lifelong Learning

As you progress through your language learning journey, remember that Market Mingle encapsulates the essence of lifelong learning. Just as each market interaction unfolds new cultural insights and linguistic discoveries, your journey in mastering Mandarin is a continuous evolution of growth, understanding, and exploration.

Market Mingle serves as a microcosm of your language journey, illustrating the profound connection between language and culture. Through conversations and bargaining, you've not only mastered practical skills but also nurtured empathy, curiosity, and a deep appreciation for the diversity of human experiences.

In the realm of Market Magic, you've transformed ordinary transactions into extraordinary encounters that transcend language barriers and cultural differences. By engaging with vendors, inquiring about goods, and negotiating with finesse, you've left an indelible mark on your path toward linguistic mastery and cultural immersion.

CHAPTER 7

Cultural Compass: Cultural Chronicles - Navigating Chinese Customs and Etiquette

Welcome to the captivating realm of Cultural Compass, where the intricate tapestry of Chinese customs and etiquette comes to life. In this chapter, we launch a mission for understanding a journey through the rich cultural landscape of China, delving into the nuances of customs, traditions, and social norms that shape everyday interactions. As you navigate this cultural compass, you'll gain profound insights into the art of respectful engagement, fostering genuine connections and demonstrating cultural sensitivity. Through this learning-oriented exploration, you'll not only deepen your understanding of Chinese society but also enhance your ability to engage meaningfully and authentically. Prepare for action to unravel the pages of Cultural Chronicles and begin a venture into a transformative trip of cross-cultural understanding.

The Heartbeat of Cultural Compass: Beyond Language

1. Culture as Context: Cultural Compass emphasizes that understanding customs and etiquette goes beyond language proficiency. Just as language is a bridge, cultural knowledge serves as the foundation for meaningful interactions, fostering empathy and connection.

2. Cultural Etiquette as a Reflection: Your ability to navigate Chinese customs reflects your respect for local values and traditions. This understanding forms the cornerstone of positive cross-cultural exchanges, leaving lasting impressions on your journey.

Cultural Customs and Everyday Etiquette

1. Greeting Gestures: Explore the various forms of greetings, from the common handshake to the traditional bow. Learn when to use each gesture and how to adapt them based on social context and the level of formality.

2. Gift-Giving Rituals: Unveil the significance of gift-giving in Chinese culture. Analyze deeply the art of selecting appropriate gifts, wrapping them with care, and presenting them with humility and respect.

3. Dining Dynamics: Immerse yourself in the world of Chinese dining etiquette. Master the use of chopsticks, understand seating arrangements, and grasp the customs of communal dining that underline the importance of unity and harmony.

Conversation and Communication Norms

1. Respectful Address: Learn the use of honorifics and formal titles when addressing individuals of different ages and social statuses. Recognize that the choice of address reflects your regard for hierarchy and mutual respect.

2. Nonverbal Communication: Understand the power of nonverbal cues, such as nodding, eye contact, and body language, in conveying respect and attentiveness. Embrace these subtle gestures to enhance the depth of your interactions.

Celebrations and Festivals

1. Lunar New Year Traditions: Explore the grandeur of Lunar New Year celebrations and their cultural significance. Learn about the customs of giving red envelopes **(hóngbāo)** and participating in festive activities that foster unity and auspicious beginnings.

2. Mid-Autumn Festival Customs: Immerse yourself in the enchanting traditions of the Mid-Autumn Festival. Discover the significance of mooncakes, lanterns, and family reunions that underscore gratitude and togetherness.

Cultural Compass in Action: Real-Life Scenarios

1. Attending Social Gatherings: Navigate through scenarios where you're invited to social gatherings. Master the art of appropriate greetings, gift-giving, and engaging in conversations that reflect your cultural awareness and respect.

2. Participating in Festivals: Step into the heart of Chinese festivals, where you'll experience firsthand the customs, traditions, and interactions that define these celebrations. Engage with locals, partake in rituals, and create lasting memories.

Cross-Cultural Empathy and Learning

1. Open-Minded Observations: Develop the skill of observing and adapting to cultural norms. Embrace the opportunity to learn from local customs, recognizing that cultural differences enrich your worldview and contribute to your personal growth.

2. Cultural Awareness in Language Learning: Acknowledge the symbiotic relationship between cultural understanding and language proficiency. By immersing yourself in Chinese customs, you enhance your ability to communicate with authenticity and depth.

Cultivating Cultural Proficiency

To amplify the enrichment of your Cultural Compass experience and cultivate cultural proficiency, consider these practical strategies:

1. Immersive Experiences: Seek opportunities for immersive cultural experiences. Attend local events, festivals, and gatherings to observe and participate in customs firsthand, deepening your connection to Chinese culture.

2. Cultural Exchange Partners: Engage in cultural exchange partnerships with native speakers. Discuss customs, share

perspectives, and ask questions to gain insights into the nuances of Chinese etiquette from those who live it daily.

3. Cultural Workshops: Participate in cultural workshops or classes that focus on Chinese customs and etiquette. These hands-on experiences provide a structured environment for learning and practicing cultural norms.

4. Cultural Literature: Explore literature, articles, and books that dig into Chinese culture. Reading about customs, traditions, and societal norms offers valuable context and expands your cultural knowledge.

Transferring Cultural Awareness Beyond Borders

1. Cultural Sensitivity in Travel: Apply your Cultural Compass skills when traveling to other countries. Adapting to local customs and showing respect for cultural differences enriches your travel experiences and fosters meaningful connections.

2. Global Cultural Etiquette: Recognize the universality of cultural awareness. Many aspects of etiquette, such as showing respect, being attentive, and practicing empathy, transcend cultural boundaries and enhance interpersonal interactions.

Unending Quest of Cultural Exploration

As you navigate the realms of Chinese customs and etiquette, remember that your journey is not confined to a single chapter. Cultural understanding is an ongoing voyage that extends beyond language learning, shaping your interactions and worldview in profound ways.

Your mastery of the Cultural Compass not only enhances your language skills but also fuels your ability to engage with people from diverse backgrounds. By embracing the values, traditions, and nuances of Chinese culture, you become a bridge that connects cultures, fosters understanding, and paves the way for meaningful relationships.

In each gesture of respect, every culturally informed conversation, and each practice of etiquette, you contribute to a world where empathy, connection, and shared appreciation for diverse traditions thrive. Your Cultural Compass serves as a beacon of cross-cultural harmony, guiding you through the labyrinth of customs and enriching your path of cultural exploration.

CHAPTER 8
Festival Revelations: Festive Flavors - Immersing in Mandarin Celebrations

Welcome to the enchanting world of Festival Revelations, where the vibrant tapestry of Mandarin celebrations unfolds before you. In this chapter, we embark upon a new venture to a journey through the heartwarming realm of festive traditions, where the joyous spirit of Mandarin-speaking cultures comes alive. Festivals serve as windows into the soul of a community, offering insights into its history, values, and shared experiences. As you study intensively into Festive Flavors, you'll immerse yourself in the colorful spectrum of Mandarin celebrations, equipping yourself with the language and cultural knowledge to participate authentically. Through this learning-oriented exploration, you'll embrace the transformative power of festivals, deepen your connection to the local communities, and foster cross-cultural understanding. Prepare for the upcoming situation to unveil the pages of Festival Revelations and set out for an unforgettable journey of cultural immersion.

Festivals as Cultural Kaleidoscopes

1. Cultural Significance: Festival Revelations emphasizes that festivals are not mere events; they are windows into the heart of a culture. By participating in celebrations, you gain a deeper understanding of the values, beliefs, and history that shape Mandarin-speaking communities.

2. Learning Through Participation: Just as language learning is experiential, cultural understanding is best achieved through participation. By immersing yourself in festivals, you learn the stories, rituals, and traditions that form the fabric of these vibrant celebrations.

Unveiling Festive Flavors: A Multitude of Celebrations

1. Lunar New Year (**春节 - Chūn Jié**): Engage deeply into the grandeur of Lunar New Year, a cornerstone of Mandarin celebrations. Learn the cultural significance of rituals, such

as the lion dance, red envelopes, and the reunion feast that symbolize new beginnings and family unity.

2. Dragon Boat Festival (端午节 - **Duān Wǔ Jié**): Immerse yourself in the rhythmic beats of Dragon Boat Festival. Discover the tale of Qu Yuan, indulge in sticky rice dumplings, and witness the exhilarating dragon boat races that exemplify unity and resilience.

3. Mid-Autumn Festival (中秋节 - **Zhōng Qiū Jié**): Explore the luminous traditions of the Mid-Autumn Festival. Delight in mooncakes, gaze at the full moon, and embrace the spirit of togetherness that echoes themes of unity, gratitude, and family bonds.

Language of Festivals: Expressions and Greetings

1. Festival Greetings: Master festival-specific greetings that encapsulate the essence of each celebration. Learn phrases like **"新年快乐" (xīn nián kuài lè) - "Happy New Year"** - and **"中秋节快乐" (zhōng qiū jié kuài lè) - "Happy Mid-Autumn Festival"** - to convey well wishes during these special occasions.

2. Participation Invitations: Discover phrases that express your enthusiasm to join in the festivities. Expressions like "我想参加" (wǒ xiǎng cān jiā) - "I'd like to participate" - showcase your eagerness to engage and experience the cultural richness of Mandarin celebrations.

Festival Traditions in Action: Real-Life Scenarios

1. Lunar New Year Delights: Step into the vibrancy of a Lunar New Year celebration, where you'll engage with locals, offer greetings, and partake in festive rituals. Immerse yourself in the festive atmosphere, spreading joy and embracing unity.

2. Dragon Boat Festival Adventures: Begin an escapade in a Dragon Boat Festival adventure, where you'll witness exhilarating races, savor traditional dumplings, and engage in conversations that uncover the historical and cultural significance of this celebration.

3. Mid-Autumn Magic: Dive into the enchantment of the Mid-Autumn Festival. Engage with locals, share mooncakes, and participate in lantern-lit gatherings that epitomize gratitude and familial bonds.

Cultural Insight and Empathy

1. Cultural Relevance: Embrace the cultural significance of festivals. By participating, you demonstrate respect for local customs and showcase your commitment to fostering cross-cultural understanding.

2. Adaptability and Respect: Recognize that festival participation may involve adapting to new experiences and practices. Approach these opportunities with an open heart, and be respectful of local traditions.

Festival Learning Beyond Borders

1. Global Festivals: Acknowledge the universality of festivals. While celebrating Mandarin festivals, draw parallels to celebrations in your own culture, fostering connections and highlighting shared values.

2. Cultural Integration: As you engage in Mandarin celebrations, embrace the integration of cultural understanding with language learning. Festivals become bridges that connect language proficiency and cross-cultural empathy.

Celebrating Unity

As we conclude our exploration of Festival Revelations, you've embarked on a journey of cultural immersion and shared experiences. By participating in Mandarin celebrations, you've not only learned the language of festivities but also discovered the universal language of joy, unity, and human connection.

Just as festivals unite communities, your participation in Festive Flavors unites cultures. Through shared celebrations, cultural understanding, and heartfelt interactions, you've woven threads of empathy and appreciation that transcend borders. As you keep moving on your linguistic and cultural voyage, remember that every festival you engage in becomes a moment of unity, leaving an indelible mark on your journey of cultural exploration and connection.

CHAPTER 9

Time-Traveling Tales: Storytelling Through Ages - Learning from Ancient Tales

Step into the enchanting realm of Time-Traveling Tales, where the echoes of ancient narratives come to life. In this chapter, enter upon a pathway to a journey through the annals of history, delving into the world of traditional stories and folktales that have captivated generations. Storytelling is a timeless art that transcends cultures, bridging the past and present through the power of words. As we explore Storytelling Through Ages, you'll uncover the treasures of wisdom, values, and cultural insights woven into these tales. Through this learning-oriented exploration, you'll not only sharpen your language skills but also gain a deeper understanding of the cultural roots and collective imagination that shape Mandarin-speaking communities. Set the groundwork to unravel the pages of Time-Traveling Tales and start a trek to a transformative journey through ancient narratives.

The Significance of Time-Traveling Tales

1. Cultural Inheritance: Time-Traveling Tales emphasizes that stories are vessels of cultural inheritance. By engaging with ancient tales, you tap into the collective memory of a culture, gaining insights into its values, beliefs, and worldview.

2. Language Enrichment: Just as stories transcend time, they enrich your language learning journey. By immersing yourself in the language of ancient tales, you expand your vocabulary, enhance your comprehension, and refine your linguistic expression.

Embarking on Time Journeys: A Glimpse of Ancient Stories

1. Journey to the West (**西游记 - Xī Yóu Jì**): Venture into the epic world of "Journey to the West," a classic tale of adventure, mythology, and spiritual quest. Uncover the

legendary exploits of the Monkey King, Tripitaka, and their companions as they journey to India.

2. Legend of the White Snake (白蛇传 - **Bái Shé Zhuàn**):

Immerse yourself in the enchanting "Legend of the White Snake," a timeless story of love, transformation, and moral dilemmas. Explore the tale of a forbidden romance between a human and a serpent spirit.

3. The Butterfly Lovers (梁山伯与祝英台 - **Liáng Shān Bó Yǔ Zhù Yīng Tái**): Discover the poignant "Butterfly Lovers," often referred to as the Chinese Romeo and Juliet. Unearth the tragic tale of **Liang Shanbo and Zhu Yingtai**, whose love defied societal norms and even death.

Language of Time-Traveling Tales: Expressions and Vocabulary

1. Ancient Idioms: Familiarize yourself with idiomatic expressions and proverbs derived from ancient tales. Learn phrases like **"情投意合" (qíng tóu yì hé) - "like-minded"** - and **"鱼与熊掌不可兼得" (yú yǔ xióng zhǎng bù kě jiān dé) - "you can't have both fish and bear's paw"** - to enrich your language with timeless wisdom.

2. Archaic Vocabulary: Embrace the use of archaic vocabulary that appears in ancient stories. Expand your linguistic repertoire with words like **"御剑" (yù jiàn) -** **"swordplay" - and "师徒" (shī tú) - "master and** **disciple"** - that transport you to the worlds of these narratives.

Tales in Action: Real-Life Scenarios

1. Retelling Legends: Step into the shoes of a storyteller as you retell ancient legends to friends or language exchange partners. Engage them with captivating narratives and embrace the opportunity to discuss cultural nuances.

2. Story Analysis: Engage in conversations that analyze the themes, characters, and moral lessons of ancient tales. Discuss the relevance of these narratives to contemporary society and share your interpretations.

Cultural Insights and Empathy

1. Cultural Context: Recognize the cultural context that shapes the narratives. By understanding the historical and societal influences on ancient tales, you deepen your appreciation for the stories' significance.

2. Empathy Through Stories: Stories are windows into the human experience. As you engage with characters' emotions and dilemmas, you foster empathy and gain insights into the shared universal values that connect us all.

Learning Beyond Ancient Tales

1. Modern Storytelling: Apply the storytelling techniques and vocabulary you learn from ancient tales to modern contexts. Enhance your ability to communicate narratives and anecdotes effectively in various social settings.

2. Literary Exploration: Explore modern literature influenced by ancient tales. Discover contemporary authors who draw inspiration from traditional narratives, creating a bridge between the past and present.

The Timeless Tapestry

As we conclude our exploration of Time-Traveling Tales, you've embarked on a journey that transcends temporal boundaries. By engaging with ancient stories, you've become a time traveler, venturing into the past to glean wisdom and cultural understanding that illuminate the present.

Just as stories are threads woven into the tapestry of cultures, your journey through Time-Traveling Tales has enriched your language learning experience. Through language and narrative, you've forged a connection with the past, a deeper understanding of the present, and a heightened sense of empathy that spans across ages.

As your expedition continues linguistic travels, may each tale you encounter serve as a reminder of the enduring power of storytelling, the shared humanity that binds us, and the limitless horizons of cultural exploration.

CHAPTER 10

Character Quest: Unraveling Characters - Your Journey into Chinese Script

Step into the captivating realm of Character Quest, where the intricate strokes of Chinese characters come to life. In this chapter, we launch into a mission for a journey that examine rigorously into the heart of the Chinese script, unveiling the art, history, and significance of characters. Chinese characters are more than just symbols; they are windows into the rich cultural tapestry of Mandarin-speaking communities. As we explore Unraveling Characters, you'll discover the beauty of written expression, enhance your language skills, and gain insights into the profound connection between characters and culture. Through this learning-oriented exploration, you'll open the door to a transformative journey into the world of Chinese script, unraveling the mysteries and embracing the elegance of characters. Make yourself set to dive into the ultimate Character Quest and forge a deep connection with the written language.

The Essence of Character Quest: Beyond Writing

1. Cultural Vessels: Character Quest emphasizes that characters are vessels of culture, encapsulating the history, values, and evolution of a society. By engaging with characters, you immerse yourself in the stories and traditions that define Mandarin-speaking communities.

2. Visual Poetry: Just as poetry conveys emotions through words, characters convey meaning through strokes. By unraveling characters, you engage with a unique form of visual poetry, enhancing your linguistic and artistic sensibilities.

Embracing the Chinese Script: Navigating Characters

1. Character Components: Discover the building blocks of Chinese characters, known as radicals and components. Learn how characters are composed, and how recognizing these elements enhances your ability to understand and remember characters.

2. Stroke Order Mastery: Master the importance of stroke order in writing characters. Understand how the correct sequence of strokes not only improves your handwriting but also aids in character recognition.

3. Pinyin and Pronunciation: Unravel the connection between characters and their pronunciation using Pinyin, the phonetic system. Learn how Pinyin helps you navigate the intricacies of tones and enhance your speaking skills.

Characters in Context: Language Integration

1. Characters in Sentences: Practice incorporating characters into sentences and short paragraphs. By using characters in context, you reinforce your understanding of grammar, syntax, and vocabulary.

2. Reading Practice: Engage with authentic texts, such as news articles, poems, and short stories, to reinforce your character recognition skills. Explore various genres and styles to expand your reading proficiency.

Cultural Insights Through Characters

1. Cultural Symbols: Recognize the cultural symbols embedded in characters. Discover characters that represent

concepts like **"家" (jiā)** - **"home"** - and **"友" (yǒu)** - **"friend,"** and explore how they reflect Chinese values and worldview.

2. Historical Significance: Explore characters with historical significance, such as those associated with ancient dynasties, philosophies, and cultural landmarks. Uncover the layers of meaning that these characters carry through time.

Character Quest in Action: Real-Life Scenarios

1. Everyday Writing: Integrate character writing into your daily routine. Practice writing shopping lists, notes, or journal entries using characters to reinforce your writing skills.

2. Digital Learning Tools: Explore digital resources and apps that offer interactive character learning. These tools provide stroke-by-stroke guidance, quizzes, and exercises to enhance your character proficiency.

Cultural Appreciation and Empathy

1. Cultural Aesthetics: Embrace the aesthetic beauty of characters. By engaging with the artistry of strokes, you gain

an appreciation for the visual elegance of Chinese script and its role in cultural expression.

2. Cultural Context: Recognize the cultural context in which characters are used. Understand how characters are woven into everyday life, from street signs to literature, and appreciate their role in preserving cultural heritage.

Learning Beyond Characters: Integration and Mastery

1. Integrated Learning: Apply character learning to other language skills. Use characters to enhance your speaking, listening, and reading abilities, creating a holistic approach to language acquisition.

2. Character Mastery: Set achievable goals for character mastery. Focus on learning a specific number of characters each week, and track your progress to build a strong foundation in written communication.

Character Expedition

As we conclude our exploration of Character Quest, you've embarked on a remarkable trip through the world of Chinese characters. By unraveling characters, you've opened the door to a new dimension of linguistic and cultural understanding.

Just as characters convey meaning, your journey through Character Quest conveys your commitment to embracing the nuances of Mandarin-speaking cultures. Through the strokes of characters, you've not only enhanced your language skills but also cultivated a profound connection with the traditions, history, and people that these characters represent.

Amid your ongoing linguistic and cultural voyage, may each character you learn be a testament to your dedication, a symbol of unity across borders, and a reminder of the infinite depth that the world of Chinese script offers.

CHAPTER 11

Expressions Explored: Everyday Expressions - Laying Foundations for Dialogue

Welcome to the illuminating journey of Expressions Explored, where the world of everyday expressions opens doors to meaningful dialogue. In this chapter, we step into a voyage through the dynamic landscape of language, focusing on the building blocks of communication - expressions. Just as a sturdy foundation supports a magnificent structure, mastering everyday expressions lays the groundwork for fluid and authentic conversations. Through this learning-oriented exploration, you'll unravel the essence of common phrases, dive deeply into their cultural nuances, and equip yourself with the tools to engage in rich, real-life dialogues. Set the stage to navigate the realm of Expressions Explored and elevate your language proficiency through the art of everyday communication.

The Essence of Expressions Explored: Beyond Words

1. Expression Elegance: Expressions Explored emphasizes that language is not only about words; it's about the art of expression. By mastering everyday phrases, you enhance your ability to convey emotions, intentions, and thoughts effectively.

2. Cultural Connection: Just as expressions are linguistic, they are cultural. By delving into everyday expressions, you gain insights into cultural norms, idiomatic expressions, and the subtleties that shape Mandarin-speaking societies.

Unraveling Everyday Expressions: Foundations of Dialogue

1. Greetings and Salutations: Explore intricately into common greetings and salutations that pave the way for interactions. Master phrases like **"你好" (nǐ hǎo) - "Hello"**

- and "早上好" (zǎo shàng hǎo) - "Good morning" - to initiate conversations with warmth.

2. Polite Requests and Offers: Explore expressions for making polite requests and extending offers. Learn phrases like "请问" (qǐng wèn) - "May I ask" - and "要不要" (yào bù yào) - "Would you like" - to engage in courteous exchanges.

3. Expressing Gratitude: Discover ways to express gratitude and appreciation. Master phrases like "谢谢" (xiè xiè) - "Thank you" - and "非常感谢" (fēi cháng gǎn xiè) - "Thank you very much" - to convey heartfelt thanks.

Cultural Insights Through Expressions

1. Cultural Values in Language: Recognize how expressions reflect cultural values. Explore phrases like "家家户户" (jiā jiā hù hù) - "every household" - and "岁岁平安" (suì suì píng ān) - "peaceful every year" - that convey familial and well-wishing sentiments.

2. Idiomatic Richness: Embrace the idiomatic nature of expressions. Learn phrases **like "一箭双雕"** (yī jiàn shuāng diāo) - **"kill two birds with one stone" - and "狐假虎威"** (hú jiǎ hǔ wēi) - **"borrowing a tiger's might"** - to appreciate the vivid imagery of idioms.

Expressions in Context: Language Integration

1. Role Play Scenarios: Engage in role-play scenarios using everyday expressions. Practice common conversational situations, such as ordering food, asking for directions, or introducing yourself, to enhance your speaking skills.

2. Conversational Partnerships: Engage in language exchange partnerships to apply expressions in real-life conversations. Role-play with native speakers or fellow learners to simulate authentic dialogues.

Language Enhancement Through Expressions

1. Vocabulary Expansion: Each expression introduces new vocabulary. Make it a practice to explore the words within expressions and incorporate them into your vocabulary.

2. Grammar Understanding: Analyze the grammar and sentence structures of expressions. By deconstructing

sentences, you deepen your understanding of grammatical rules and syntax.

Expressions Explored in Action: Real-Life Scenarios

1. Café Conversations: Step into a café scenario where you'll utilize everyday expressions to order coffee, ask about the menu, and engage in casual conversations with locals or fellow learners.

2. Market Interactions: Immerse yourself in a bustling market setting, where you'll apply expressions to negotiate prices, inquire about products, and engage in friendly exchanges with vendors.

Practical Application and Empathy

1. Cultural Adaptation: Recognize the adaptability of expressions across cultures. As you use Mandarin expressions, appreciate their universal power in building connections and showing respect.

2. Empathy Through Expressions: Engage with the emotions embedded in expressions. Understand the nuances of phrases like **"你怎么了"** (**nǐ zěn me le**) - **"What's wrong with**

you" - and **"好久不见"** (**hǎo jiǔ bù jiàn**) - **"Long time no see"** - to empathize and connect on a deeper level.

Learning Beyond Expressions: Integration and Fluency

1. Expression Expansion: Apply the expressions you learn to various contexts. Experiment with using expressions in different social settings, such as formal and informal conversations, to refine your language versatility.

2. Contextual Adaptation: Adapt expressions to reflect your personal experiences and style. Modify expressions to convey your unique voice while staying true to their core meanings.

Continued Exploration

As you pilot the realm of Expressions Explored, your journey is far from over. Everyday expressions are the threads that weave the fabric of authentic dialogue, bridging the gap between languages and cultures.

Through your mastery of these linguistic gems, you become a storyteller, a connector, and a cultural ambassador. Each expression you use is a testament to your dedication to meaningful communication and your commitment to fostering cross-cultural understanding.

In the span of your linguistic and cultural voyage, may every expression you learn be a stepping stone toward fluency, an invitation to connect, and a reminder of the transformative power of language in building bridges between hearts.

Cultivating Expression Proficiency

To enrich and deepen your Expressions Explored experience and cultivate expression proficiency, consider these practical strategies:

1. Contextual Role-Play: Create and participate in contextual role-play scenarios with fellow learners or language exchange partners. Simulate real-life situations to practice using expressions in different contexts.

2. Daily Expression Challenge: Challenge yourself to incorporate a specific expression into your daily conversations or written communication. This practice helps reinforce your memory and usage of expressions.

3. Multimedia Engagement: Watch movies, TV shows, or podcasts in Mandarin and pay attention to how characters

use everyday expressions. This exposure to authentic language use enhances your comprehension and natural use of expressions.

4. Expression Journal: Maintain an expression journal where you record new expressions you encounter. Include the context, meaning, and example sentences for each expression to create a valuable reference.

Transferring Expression Knowledge Beyond Conversation

1. Expression Writing: Utilize expressions in your writing practice. Craft short stories, essays, or even social media posts that incorporate expressions to enhance your written communication skills.

2. Artistic Expression: Use expressions as inspiration for creative projects, such as poetry, artwork, or photography. Express the meanings and emotions conveyed by expressions through different artistic mediums.

Unceasing Adventure of Expression Exploration

While you steer through the diverse world of everyday expressions, remember that your journey is an ongoing adventure. Expressions Explored symbolizes the perpetual exploration of language nuances, cultural connections, and the art of communication.

By mastering everyday expressions, you not only lay the foundations for effective dialogue but also become a bridge builder, fostering connections across linguistic and cultural boundaries. Each expression you learn becomes a tool of expression, a vessel of meaning, and an invitation to engage in meaningful interactions.

Along the path of your linguistic and cultural excursion, may each expression you incorporate into your language repertoire be a testament to your commitment to effective communication, a testament to your cultural empathy, and a reminder of the limitless possibilities that expressions offer in your quest for linguistic mastery.

CHAPTER 12

Idioms Illuminated: Idiomatic Insights - Embracing Figurative Language

Step into the enchanting realm of Idioms Illuminated, where the colorful tapestry of figurative language unfolds before your eyes. In this chapter, we begin a voyage to a captivating journey through the world of idioms, exploring their richness, cultural significance, and linguistic intricacies. Idioms are the gems of language, encapsulating vivid imagery, cultural nuances, and nuanced meanings. As we unearth into Idiomatic Insights, you'll discover the art of embracing figurative language, enhance your language skills, and gain a deeper understanding of the layers of expression that define Mandarin-speaking cultures.

Through this learning-oriented exploration, you'll unveil the charm of idiomatic phrases, master their usage, and step into the world of imaginative communication. Ready up your resources to illuminate your language journey with the brilliance of idioms and their illuminating insights.

The Essence of Idioms Illuminated: Beyond Literalism

1. Figurative Marvels: Idioms Illuminated emphasizes that idioms are more than words; they are windows into cultural expressions and creative language use. By mastering idiomatic phrases, you enhance your ability to convey complex meanings and emotions.

2. Cultural Treasure Trove: Just as idioms are linguistic, they are cultural. By immersing yourself in idiomatic expressions, you unlock cultural references, historical allusions, and the poetic tapestry that defines Mandarin-speaking communities.

Unveiling Idiomatic Insights: The Language of Imagery

1. Animal Idioms: Explore idioms featuring animals as metaphors. Learn phrases **like "狐假虎威" (hú jiǎ hǔ wēi) - "borrowing a tiger's might" - and "一箭双雕" (yī jiàn**

shuāng diāo) - **"kill two birds with one stone"** - to unravel the vivid imagery of animal-related idioms.

2. Weather Idioms: Dive into idioms inspired by weather phenomena. Master expressions like **"如日中天" (rú rì zhōng tiān) - "like the midday sun" - and "春意盎然" (chūn yì àng rán) - "full of the joy of spring"** - to explore the poetic beauty of weather-based idioms.

3. Body Idioms: Engage with idioms that use body parts to convey meaning. Learn phrases like **"眼前一亮" (yǎn qián yī liàng) - "eyes light up" - and "心口如一" (xīn kǒu rú yī) - "saying what's in one's heart"** - to unravel the imaginative language of body-related idioms.

Cultural Insights Through Idioms

1. Historical Roots: Recognize the historical origins of idioms. Explore idioms with connections to ancient stories, literature, and historical events to gain insights into their cultural significance.

2. Wisdom in Metaphor: Embrace the wisdom embedded in idioms. Learn idioms **like "授人以鱼不如授人以渔" (shòu**

rén yǐ yú bù rú shòu rén yǐ yú) - "give a man a fish and you feed him for a day; teach a man to fish and you feed him for a lifetime" - to uncover their philosophical and moral teachings.

Idioms in Action: Language Integration

1. Storytelling with Idioms: Craft short stories or anecdotes that incorporate idioms. This practice enhances your narrative skills while reinforcing your understanding of idiomatic expressions.

2. Conversational Challenges: Engage in language challenges where you use idiomatic phrases in conversations. Engage in discussions, debates, or casual talks while incorporating idioms to enrich your language use.

Language Enrichment Through Idioms

1. Vocabulary Enhancement: Idioms introduce unique vocabulary and expressions. Investigate the meanings of individual words within idioms to expand your vocabulary repertoire.

2. Grammar Insights: Analyze the grammar and sentence structures of idiomatic phrases. By dissecting idioms, you deepen your comprehension of sentence formation and syntactical patterns

Idioms Illuminated in Action: Real-Life Scenarios

1. Meeting Friends: Immerse yourself in a scenario where you engage in lively conversations with friends, using idioms to add color and depth to your dialogue.

2. Job Interview: Step into a job interview setting, where you demonstrate your language prowess by incorporating idiomatic expressions to convey confidence and professionalism.

Practical Application and Cultural Sensitivity

1. Cultural Nuances: Recognize the cultural sensitivities in using idioms. Understand the contexts in which idioms are appropriate, ensuring your communication is respectful and culturally informed.

2. Empathy Through Idioms: Engage with the emotions and experiences captured in idioms. Grasp the essence of phrases like **"一帆风顺" (yī fān fēng shùn) - "smooth sailing"** -

and "人山人海" (rén shān rén hǎi) - "huge crowds of people" - to connect on a deeper level.

Learning Beyond Idioms: Integration and Expression Mastery

1. Idiomatic Conversations: Integrate idioms into different conversational settings. Explore both formal and informal contexts, from business meetings to casual chats, to enhance your versatility in using idiomatic language.

2. Idiom Interpretation: Practice interpreting idioms in context. Engage in discussions that analyze the meanings and implications of idiomatic phrases, refining your comprehension and analytical skills.

Continued Discovery

As you steer through the captivating world of idioms, your journey is a continuous exploration. Idioms Illuminated represents an ongoing quest to master the art of figurative language, uncover cultural wisdom, and express yourself with eloquence.

By embracing idiomatic expressions, you become a storyteller, a poet, and a cultural enthusiast. Each idiom you learn opens a window to the imaginative realm of language and contributes to your ability to connect, express, and engage.

Through your persistent linguistic and cultural sojourn, may each idiom you encounter be a source of inspiration, a bridge between languages, and a reminder of the vibrant tapestry that idiomatic expressions weave into the fabric of communication.

Cultivating Idiomatic Proficiency

To elevate the richness of your Idioms Illuminated experience and cultivate idiomatic proficiency, consider these practical strategies:

1. Daily Idiom Challenge: Challenge yourself to use a different idiom in your daily conversations or writing. This exercise not only reinforces your understanding but also encourages creative language use.

2. Idiom Exploration Groups: Form or join language groups focused on exploring idioms. Collaborate with fellow learners to discuss, analyze, and use idiomatic expressions in various contexts.

3. Idiomatic Storytelling: Create short stories, dialogues, or poems that incorporate multiple idioms. This creative exercise enhances your mastery of idiomatic language while fostering your storytelling skills.

4. Language Exchange with Idioms: Engage in language exchange partnerships specifically aimed at practicing idioms. Share idiomatic expressions from your native language while learning those from your partner's language.

Transferring Idiomatic Knowledge Beyond Language

1. Creative Writing: Use idiomatic expressions as prompts for creative writing projects. Develop short stories, poems, or essays inspired by the meanings and imagery of idioms.

2. Artistic Interpretation: Embrace idioms as sources of artistic inspiration. Create visual artworks, sculptures, or multimedia projects that convey the essence of idiomatic phrases.

Forever Wander of Idiomatic Exploration

In your journey to navigate the world of idioms, remember that your journey is an ongoing adventure of discovery. Idioms Illuminated symbolizes the continuous exploration of language's poetic nuances, cultural insights, and the artistry of expression.

By mastering idiomatic expressions, you not only wield linguistic gems but also become an ambassador of creativity, a connector of cultures, and a connoisseur of language's colorful palette. Each idiom you learn is an invitation to unravel layers of meaning, a key to unlocking cultural contexts, and a reminder of the limitless possibilities that language offers.

During your unceasing linguistic and cultural campaign, may each idiom you embrace be a testament to your dedication to linguistic artistry, a bridge to understanding diverse cultures, and a beacon of the profound impact that idiomatic language has on shaping rich and vibrant communication.

CHAPTER 13

Café Conversations: Café Chitchat - Conversations and Connections

S tep into the inviting ambiance of Café Conversations, where the aroma of freshly brewed coffee mingles with the art of dialogue. In this chapter, we launch a mission to a delightful journey through the world of café interactions, discovering the nuances of language, culture, and connection. Café Conversations is more than just ordering a drink; it's an exploration of interpersonal communication, social dynamics, and the joy of engaging with others. Through this learning-oriented exploration, you'll unravel the intricacies of café chitchat, master the art of ordering, and forge connections that extend beyond the coffee cup. Make yourself prepared to immerse yourself in the heart of Café Conversations and elevate your language proficiency through the art of meaningful interactions.

The Essence of Café Conversations: Beyond Beverages

1. Societal Reflections: Café Conversations underscores that cafes are microcosms of society, reflecting cultural norms, social interactions, and human connections. By mastering café interactions, you enhance your ability to navigate real-life social settings.

2. Cultural Elegance: Just as cafes are gathering places, they are also cultural hubs. By getting engaged in café conversations, you absorb local customs, etiquette, and the unspoken language of coffee culture.

Unraveling Café Chitchat: Language and Interaction

1. Ordering and Preferences: Research meticulously into the art of ordering beverages and food items. Master phrases **like "我想要" (wǒ xiǎng yào) - "I would like" - and "请给我" (qǐng gěi wǒ) - "please give me"** - to navigate café menus with confidence.

2. Asking Questions: Explore the art of asking questions and seeking information. Learn phrases like **"这是什么" (zhè shì shén me) - "What is this?" - and "请问有没有" (qǐng wèn yǒu méi yǒu) - "Do you have"** - to engage in informative conversations with café staff.

3. Expressing Preferences: Discover ways to express your preferences and customize your order. Master phrases like **"我喜欢" (wǒ xǐ huān) - "I like" - and "少放/多放" (shǎo fàng/duō fàng) - "less/more"** - to tailor your beverage just the way you like it.

Cultural Insights Through Café Conversations

1. Coffee Culture: Recognize the cultural significance of coffee and cafes. Explore phrases like **"一杯咖啡" (yī bēi kā fēi) - "a cup of coffee" - and "咖啡因" (kā fēi yīn) - "caffeine"** - to understand the role of coffee in modern lifestyles.

2. Social Norms: Embrace the social dynamics of café interactions. Learn phrases like **"请坐" (qǐng zuò) - "please**

have a seat" - and "慢慢喝" (màn màn hē) - "enjoy your drink" - to navigate social cues and interactions.

Café Conversations in Action: Language Integration

1. Role-Play Scenarios: Engage in role-play scenarios that mimic café interactions. Practice ordering, asking questions, and engaging in casual conversations to refine your language skills.

2. Real Café Visits: Apply your café conversation skills in real-life settings. Visit local cafes and engage in genuine interactions with café staff, fellow customers, or language exchange partners.

Language Enhancement Through Café Chitchat

1. Vocabulary Expansion: Each café conversation introduces new vocabulary related to beverages, food, and social interactions. Explore the meanings and usage of these words to enrich your vocabulary.

2. Polite Communication: Analyze the nuances of polite communication. Understand expressions like "请" (qǐng) -

"please" - and **"谢谢"** (xiè xiè) - **"thank you"** - to ensure respectful and courteous interactions.

Café Conversations in Action: Real-Life Scenarios

1. Meeting a Friend: Immerse yourself in a scenario where you meet a friend at a café, engage in light-hearted banter, and create memorable moments through conversation.

2. Meeting a Colleague: Step into a café setting where you meet a colleague for a discussion, showcasing your ability to communicate professionally and effectively.

Practical Application and Social Sensitivity

1. Cultural Adaptation: Recognize the cultural norms of café interactions. Understand how expressions like **"坐吧" (zuò ba) - "please have a seat"** - and **"慢慢喝" (màn màn hē) - "enjoy your drink"** - reflect social hospitality.

2. Empathy Through Conversations: Engage with the emotions and connections fostered through café conversations. Grasp the essence of phrases like **"来一杯" (lái yī bēi) - "bring a cup"** - and **"辛苦了" (xīn kǔ le) - "you've worked hard"** - to connect on a deeper level.

Learning Beyond Café Conversations: Integration and Connection Mastery

1. Diverse Cafés: Practice café conversations in different café settings. Explore casual cafés, upscale establishments, and cultural-themed coffee shops to adapt your language use.

2. Cross-Cultural Cafés: Engage in language exchanges in international cafés. Connect with people from various linguistic backgrounds while practicing café conversations in a multicultural context.

Continued Interaction

In your effort to lead the realm of Café Conversations, your journey is a perpetual exploration. Café Chitchat represents an ongoing quest to master the art of dialogue, build connections, and create shared experiences.

By immersing yourself in café conversations, you become a cultural explorer, a social connector, and a confident communicator. Each café interaction is an opportunity to learn, share, and create lasting connections that transcend linguistic and cultural barriers.

Throughout your forward linguistic and cultural excursion, may each café conversation you engage in be a reminder of the warmth of human connection, a celebration of shared moments, and a testament to the profound impact that meaningful dialogue has on fostering understanding and camaraderie.

Cultivating Café Conversation Proficiency

For added texture to your Café Conversations experience and cultivate café conversation proficiency, consider these practical strategies:

1. Café Visits: Regularly visit local cafes to practice your conversation skills. Challenge yourself to engage in interactions with café staff and fellow patrons, gradually building your confidence.

2. Café Journal: Maintain a café journal where you record your café experiences, conversations, and new vocabulary. Reflect on each interaction to identify areas for improvement.

3. Cultural Research: Explore the coffee culture of different regions. Learn about traditional beverages, café etiquette,

and common customs to enhance your cultural awareness during café conversations.

4. Language Exchange Cafés: Seek out language exchange events hosted in cafes. These gatherings provide an excellent opportunity to engage in conversations with native speakers and fellow learners.

Transferring Café Conversation Knowledge Beyond Cafes

1. Creative Writing: Incorporate café conversations into your creative writing projects. Develop short stories, dialogues, or scenes that showcase authentic café interactions.

2. Café-inspired Art: Create artworks, illustrations, or photography inspired by café conversations. Capture the essence of these interactions through visual mediums.

Timeless Passage of Conversation Connection

While managing your way through the realm of Café Conversations, remember that your journey is a continuous exploration of connection and communication. Café Chitchat symbolizes the ongoing quest to bridge linguistic gaps, foster social bonds, and embrace cultural diversity.

By becoming active in café conversations, you not only order beverages; you order experiences, stories, and shared moments. Each interaction becomes a part of your linguistic tapestry, contributing to your ability to connect, converse, and create relationships that enrich your life.

During your ongoing linguistic and cultural quest, may each café conversation you initiate be a reminder of the power of language to unite, a celebration of the diverse flavors of human interaction, and a testament to the lasting impact that genuine conversations have in building bridges between individuals and cultures.

CHAPTER 14

Doctor Dialogues: Health Talks - Navigating Medical Conversations

Welcome to the informative realm of Doctor Dialogues, where language becomes a vital tool for understanding and navigating the world of healthcare. In this chapter, we enter into a crucial journey through medical conversations, equipping you with the language skills to communicate effectively with medical professionals, express health concerns, and seek medical advice. Doctor Dialogues is not just about words; it's about empowerment, knowledge, and the ability to advocate for your well-being. Through this learning-oriented exploration, you'll uncover the intricacies of medical language, master health-related expressions, and develop the confidence to engage in meaningful conversations with healthcare providers. Get into position to immerse yourself in the realm of Health Talks and elevate your language proficiency for a healthier and more informed life.

The Essence of Doctor Dialogues: Beyond Symptoms

1. Health Empowerment: Doctor Dialogues underscores that effective communication in medical settings empowers individuals to take charge of their health. By mastering medical conversations, you enhance your ability to access quality healthcare and make informed decisions.

2. Cultural Sensitivity: Just as healthcare is a universal concern, it is also culturally diverse. By engaging in doctor dialogues, you learn to navigate cultural norms, medical practices, and the nuances of seeking healthcare in different contexts.

Unraveling Health Talks: Language and Medical Interaction

1. Expressing Symptoms: Analyze in great detail the art of describing health symptoms. Master phrases like "我感觉不舒服" (wǒ gǎn jué bù shū fú) - "I don't feel well" - and "

头疼/发烧" (tóu téng/fā shāo) - "headache/fever" - to convey your health concerns accurately.

2. Asking Questions: Explore how to ask questions during medical consultations. Learn phrases like **"这是什么症状"** (zhè shì shén me zhèng zhuàng) - **"What are these symptoms?"** - and **"怎么办"** (zěn me bàn) - **"What should I do?"** - to seek guidance from medical professionals.

3. Expressing Concerns: Discover ways to express your medical concerns and preferences. Master phrases **like "我有过敏"** (wǒ yǒu guò mǐn) - **"I have allergies"** - and **"我想避免用药"** (wǒ xiǎng bì miǎn yòng yào) - **"I want to avoid medication"** - to engage in informed medical discussions.

Cultural Insights Through Health Talks

1. Medical Etiquette: Recognize the importance of medical etiquette. Explore phrases like **"请问您有什么症状"** (qǐng wèn nín yǒu shén me zhèng zhuàng) - **"May I ask about**

your symptoms?" - and "我们会尽力帮助您" (wǒ men huì jìn lì bāng zhù nín) - "We will do our best to assist you" - to understand the courteous language of medical interactions.

2. Treatment Approaches: Embrace the diversity of medical practices. Learn phrases like "中医" (zhōng yī) - "traditional Chinese medicine" - and "西医" (xī yī) - "Western medicine" - to appreciate the cultural and medical choices available.

Health Talks in Action: Language Integration

1. Role-Play Scenarios: Engage in role-play scenarios that simulate medical consultations. Practice expressing symptoms, asking questions, and discussing treatment options to refine your language skills.

2. Medical Simulations: Participate in medical simulations with language exchange partners. Simulate doctor-patient interactions to enhance your ability to engage in meaningful medical conversations.

Language Enhancement Through Health Talks

1. Vocabulary Expansion: Each health conversation introduces new medical vocabulary and terminology. Investigate the meanings of medical terms to build a comprehensive health-related vocabulary.

2. Communication Clarity: Analyze the clarity of your communication. Understand expressions like **"可以再说一遍吗"** (kě yǐ zài shuō yī biàn ma) - "Can you say that again?" - and **"我不太明白"** (wǒ bù tài míng bái) - "I don't quite understand"** - to ensure effective communication with medical professionals.

Health Talks in Action: Real-Life Scenarios

1. Doctor's Appointment: Immerse yourself in a scenario where you visit a doctor's office, engage in a consultation, and effectively communicate your health concerns.

2. Pharmacy Visit: Step into a pharmacy setting where you seek medication, discuss dosage instructions, and clarify any medical queries with the pharmacist.

Practical Application and Personal Advocacy

1. Cultural Adaptation: Recognize the cultural nuances of seeking healthcare. Understand how expressions like **"请问有预约吗"** (qǐng wèn yǒu yù yuē ma) - **"Do you have an appointment?"** - and **"我想咨询一下"** (wǒ xiǎng zī xún yī xià) - **"I would like to ask for advice"** - reflect cultural respect and consideration.

2. Empathy Through Health Talks: Engage with the emotions and health-related concerns conveyed through medical conversations. Grasp the essence of phrases **like "希望您早日康复"** (xī wàng nín zǎo rì kāng fù) - **"Wishing you a speedy recovery"** - to express empathy and care.

Learning Beyond Health Talks: Empowerment and Advocacy

1. Health Literacy: Extend your health knowledge through research. Study medical conditions, treatment options, and preventive measures to become a more informed advocate for your well-being.

2. Translation Practice: Engage in translating medical documents or articles. Practice translating health-related

information to enhance your language skills and medical literacy.

Continued Health Conversation

While you proceed through the realm of Doctor Dialogues, your journey is a continuous pursuit of health literacy and effective communication. Health Talks represents an ongoing quest to master the language of medical interactions, advocate for your health needs, and make informed choices.

By immersing yourself in health conversations, you become a health advocate, a knowledgeable patient, and a confident communicator. Each health dialogue is an opportunity to learn, express, and collaborate towards better health outcomes.

Throughout your ongoing linguistic and health-oriented venture, may each medical conversation you engage in be a reminder of the importance of effective communication in healthcare, a celebration of your role in shaping your well-being, and a testament to the transformative impact that informed and empowered conversations have on health and quality of life.

Cultivating Health Conversation Proficiency

To heighten the depth of your Doctor Dialogues experience and cultivate health conversation proficiency, consider these practical strategies:

1. Health Research: Dive into health-related resources. Explore medical websites, articles, and publications in Mandarin to enhance your medical vocabulary and knowledge.

2. Medical Role-Plays: Engage in frequent medical role-play scenarios. Practice different medical situations, such as doctor's visits, pharmacy interactions, and emergency situations, to build your confidence and fluency.

3. Health Vocabulary Cards: Create flashcards with medical terms and phrases. Regularly review and test yourself to reinforce your vocabulary and improve your retention.

4. Translation Exercises: Translate health-related texts from your native language to Mandarin. This exercise sharpens your translation skills and deepens your understanding of medical terminology.

Transferring Health Conversation Knowledge Beyond Healthcare

1. Health Journaling: Maintain a health journal in Mandarin. Record your daily health observations, symptoms, and experiences to enhance your ability to describe health-related matters.

2. Health Seminars and Workshops: Attend health-related seminars or workshops conducted in Mandarin. Participate in discussions and engage with experts to expand your medical knowledge.

Eternal Ramble of Health Advocacy

As you maneuver through the world of Doctor Dialogues, your journey is an ongoing commitment to health advocacy, informed decision-making, and effective communication. Health Talks symbolizes the continuous pursuit of health and language literacy, resulting in a more empowered and confident approach to healthcare.

By dabbling into health conversations, you become a participant in your own well-being, a communicator of health concerns, and a supporter of informed healthcare choices. Each health dialogue you initiate is a step towards better health outcomes, improved patient-doctor relationships, and an increased sense of control over your health journey.

In the midst of your linguistic and health-oriented pioneering, may each health conversation you engage in be a reminder of your capacity to take charge of your health, a celebration of your role in shaping your wellness narrative, and a testament to the positive impact that effective health communication has on overall quality of life.

CHAPTER 15
Cultural Connection: Cultural Kaleidoscope - Understanding Chinese Traditions

Welcome to the vibrant realm of Cultural Connection, where language and culture intertwine to create a tapestry of understanding and appreciation. In this chapter, we venture forth into a captivating journey through Chinese traditions, exploring the rich heritage, customs, and rituals that shape the cultural landscape. Cultural Connection goes beyond words; it's an immersion into the heart of a nation's identity, a journey that unveils the essence of cultural expressions, and a doorway to building meaningful relationships.

Through this learning-oriented exploration, you'll plunge deeply into the intricacies of Chinese traditions, master cultural terminology, and develop a profound connection with the essence of Chinese culture. Set yourself up to uncover the mosaic of Cultural Kaleidoscope and elevate your language proficiency through the beauty of cultural understanding.

The Essence of Cultural Connection: Beyond Language

1. Cultural Enrichment: Cultural Connection highlights that language learning extends beyond words to encompass cultural depth. By understanding Chinese traditions, you enrich your language skills and foster cross-cultural empathy.

2. Cross-Cultural Communication: Just as language is a bridge, culture is the foundation. By venturing into cultural connection, you cultivate the ability to communicate effectively and respectfully across cultural boundaries.

Unraveling Cultural Kaleidoscope: Language and Traditions

1. Festivals and Celebrations: Dig deeply into the art of understanding Chinese festivals and celebrations. Master

terms like **"春节"** **(chūn jié)** - **"Spring Festival"** - and **"中秋节"** **(zhōng qiū jié)** - **"Mid-Autumn Festival"** - to explore the vibrancy of traditional festivities.

2. Cultural Symbols: Explore the meanings behind Chinese cultural symbols. Learn about **"龙"** **(lóng)** - **"dragon"** - and **"凤凰"** **(fèng huáng)** - **"phoenix"** - to uncover the profound symbolism embedded in Chinese culture.

3. Etiquette and Customs: Discover the nuances of Chinese etiquette and customs. Master phrases **like "鞠躬" (jū gōng)** - **"bowing" - and "请坐" (qǐng zuò) - "please have a seat"** - to navigate social interactions with cultural sensitivity.

Cultural Insights Through Cultural Connection

1. Historical Significance: Recognize the historical roots of Chinese traditions. Explore the significance of cultural practices **like "拜年" (bài nián) - "New Year greetings" - and "传统婚礼" (chuán tǒng hūn lǐ) - "traditional wedding ceremony"** - to understand their importance in Chinese heritage.

2. Philosophical Wisdom: Embrace the philosophical underpinnings of Chinese culture. Learn about concepts like **"仁" (rén) - "benevolence" - and "道" (dào) - "the way"** - to grasp the profound wisdom that guides cultural values.

Cultural Kaleidoscope in Action: Language Integration

1. Cultural Conversations: Engage in role-play scenarios that revolve around Chinese traditions. Practice discussing festivals, customs, and cultural symbols to refine your language skills.

2. Cultural Presentations: Prepare and deliver presentations about specific Chinese traditions. Share insights about festivals, rituals, and cultural practices to enhance your language proficiency and cultural knowledge.

Language Enhancement Through Cultural Connection

1. Vocabulary Expansion: Each cultural connection introduces new vocabulary related to Chinese traditions. Investigate the meanings and significance of these terms to build a comprehensive cultural vocabulary.

2. Cultural Terminology: Analyze the linguistic nuances of cultural terminology. Understand expressions like "传统"

(chuán tǒng) - "tradition" - and "文化" (wén huà) - "culture" - to effectively convey cultural concepts.

Cultural Kaleidoscope in Action: Real-Life Scenarios

1. Cultural Gathering: Immerse yourself in a scenario where you attend a cultural gathering, engaging in discussions about Chinese traditions and sharing your insights.

2. Cultural Exchange: Step into a cultural exchange event, where you interact with Chinese natives or fellow learners, celebrating diversity and exploring shared cultural interests.

Practical Application and Cross-Cultural Sensitivity

1. Cultural Adaptation: Recognize the importance of cultural respect. Understand how expressions like **"我很尊重你们的传统" (wǒ hěn zūn zhòng nǐ men de chuán tǒng) - "I respect your traditions"** - and **"请告诉我更多" (qǐng gào sù wǒ gèng duō) - "please tell me more"** - reflect cultural openness and curiosity.

2. Cultural Exchange Through Language: Engage in language exchange partnerships with native Chinese

speakers. Discuss traditions, festivals, and cultural nuances to enhance your cross-cultural understanding.

Learning Beyond Cultural Connection: Cultural Insight and Empathy

1. Cultural Immersion: Immerse yourself in Chinese cultural experiences. Attend cultural events, workshops, or performances to deepen your connection with Chinese traditions.

2. Cultural Reflection: Engage in cultural reflection exercises. Write essays or journals about your experiences with Chinese traditions, expressing your insights and personal growth.

Continued Cultural Connection

While you forge ahead with your way through the captivating world of Cultural Connection, your journey is an ongoing exploration of cultural empathy, understanding, and appreciation. Cultural Kaleidoscope symbolizes the perpetual quest to bridge cultural gaps, foster cross-cultural friendships, and celebrate the mosaic of human diversity.

By partaking actively in cultural connections, you become a cultural ambassador, a global citizen, and a bridge between cultures. Each cultural insight you gain is an opportunity to learn, share, and create connections that transcend linguistic and geographical boundaries.

Along your persistent linguistic and cross-cultural tour, may each cultural connection you embrace be a reminder of the beauty of diversity, a celebration of shared humanity, and a testament to the transformative power of understanding and appreciating different cultures.

Cultivating Cultural Connection Proficiency

To infuse more richness into your Cultural Connection experience and cultivate cultural connection proficiency, consider these practical strategies:

1. Cultural Workshops: Attend cultural workshops or events focused on Chinese traditions. Engage in hands-on activities, such as traditional art, cooking, or music, to immerse yourself in the cultural experience.

2. Cultural Mentorship: Seek guidance from individuals well-versed in Chinese traditions. Connect with mentors,

cultural enthusiasts, or local experts who can provide deeper insights into the cultural nuances.

3. Cultural Exploration Groups: Form or join groups dedicated to exploring Chinese traditions. Collaborate with fellow learners to discuss, analyze, and celebrate various aspects of Chinese culture.

4. Cultural Immersion Trips: Plan trips to China to experience the traditions firsthand. Participate in local festivals, visit historical sites, and engage with the local community to gain authentic cultural insights.

Transferring Cultural Connection Knowledge Beyond Cultural Contexts

1. Artistic Expression: Use Chinese cultural elements as inspiration for creative projects. Create artworks, crafts, or performances that pay homage to Chinese traditions and symbolism.

2. Cultural Exchange Events: Organize or participate in cultural exchange events. Share your understanding of Chinese traditions with others and learn about their cultural backgrounds in return.

Perpetual Excursion of Cultural Understanding

As you navigate the realm of Cultural Connection, never forget that your adventure is an everlasting exploration of cultural diversity, empathy, and global unity. Cultural Kaleidoscope represents the continuous quest to transcend borders, forge connections, and embrace the richness of the world's cultures.

By committing to cultural connections, you not only learn about traditions; you learn about humanity, empathy, and the universal threads that bind us all. Each cultural insight you gain becomes a window into a different way of life, a mirror that reflects our shared experiences, and a doorway to meaningful connections with people from all walks of life.

As you persist in your linguistic and cultural exploration, may each cultural connection you make be a reminder of the beauty of cultural diversity, a celebration of the tapestry of human experiences, and a testament to the profound impact that cross-cultural understanding has in fostering global harmony.

CHAPTER 16

Short Story Magic: Crafting Narratives - Learning Through Stories

Step into the enchanting world of Short Story Magic, where language becomes a canvas for creativity and storytelling takes center stage. In this chapter, we get out on an immersive journey through the realm of narratives, exploring the art of crafting and understanding short stories in Mandarin. Short Story Magic is more than just tales; it's a gateway to language mastery, cognitive development, and cultural insights. Through this learning-oriented exploration, you'll unravel the elements of storytelling, master narrative techniques, and cultivate a deep connection with Mandarin language and culture. Standby to dive into the world of Crafting Narratives and elevate your language proficiency through the power of storytelling.

The Essence of Short Story Magic: Beyond Words

1. Cognitive Engagement: Short Story Magic emphasizes that storytelling engages cognitive faculties, enhancing language retention and comprehension. By immersing yourself in short stories, you stimulate your mind and foster active language learning.

2. Cultural Reflection: Just as stories are cultural mirrors, they also provide windows into different worlds. By exploring short stories, you gain insights into Chinese perspectives, values, and societal dynamics.

Unraveling Crafting Narratives: Language and Imagination

1. Character Development: Immerse yourself deeply into the art of character creation. Master descriptive language and personality traits, using phrases like **"她是一个聪明的女孩" (tā shì yī gè cōng míng de nǚ hái)** - "She is a clever girl" - to bring characters to life.

2. Plot Building: Explore the intricacies of plot construction. Learn phrases **like "一天，有一只小鸟飞到了村子里" (yī tiān, yǒu yī zhī xiǎo niǎo fēi dào le cūn zi lǐ) - "One day,** a little bird flew into the village" - to create engaging and captivating storylines.

3. Setting and Atmosphere: Discover how to evoke settings and atmosphere through language. Master descriptive phrases **like "在一个古老的庙宇里" (zài yī gè gǔ lǎo de miào yǔ lǐ) - "In an ancient temple"** - to transport readers to vivid and immersive environments.

Cultural Insights Through Crafting Narratives

1. Historical Context: Recognize the historical context embedded in narratives. Explore phrases like **"在古代的中国" (zài gǔ dài de zhōng guó) - "In ancient China" - and "那个时候" (nà gè shí hòu) - "at that time"** - to understand the temporal and cultural backdrop of stories.

2. Social Dynamics: Embrace the portrayal of societal norms and interactions. Learn about expressions like **"他们是一对**

好朋友" (tā men shì yī duì hǎo péng yǒu) - **"They are good friends"** - to grasp the dynamics of relationships in different contexts.

Crafting Narratives in Action: Language Integration

1. Storytelling Workshops: Engage in storytelling workshops or creative writing exercises. Practice developing characters, constructing plots, and describing settings to refine your language skills.

2. Narrative Comprehension: Analyze and discuss existing short stories. Participate in narrative comprehension activities, summarizing plots, and interpreting character motivations to enhance your language proficiency.

Language Enhancement Through Crafting Narratives

1. Vocabulary Enrichment: Each short story introduces new vocabulary and expressions. Explore the meanings and usage of these words to expand your lexicon and storytelling capabilities.

2. Language Fluency: Analyze the flow and coherence of language in narratives. Understand expressions like **"然后"**

(rán hòu) - "then" - and "最后" (zuì hòu) - "finally" - to enhance the fluidity of your storytelling.

Crafting Narratives in Action: Original Stories

1. Personal Narratives: Immerse yourself in crafting personal narratives. Develop short stories based on your experiences, interests, or imaginative scenarios to practice storytelling techniques.

2. Cultural Tales: Step into the realm of Chinese culture by creating stories that revolve around cultural elements, traditions, or historical events. This exercise deepens your understanding of both language and culture.

Practical Application and Creative Expression

1. Adaptation and Translation: Adapt or translate existing stories into Mandarin. Practice retaining the essence of the original narrative while integrating the nuances of the Chinese language.

2. Multimedia Storytelling: Experiment with multimedia storytelling. Create audio recordings, animations, or visual presentations to accompany your narratives and enhance your language learning experience.

Learning Beyond Crafting Narratives: Imagination and Connection

1. Literary Exploration: Engage with Chinese literature. Read short stories, folktales, or modern fiction to expand your exposure to narrative styles and language use.

2. Interpretive Discussions: Participate in interpretive discussions about stories. Engage in conversations that analyze themes, character development, and cultural motifs to deepen your narrative understanding.

Continued Storytelling Mastery

As you navigate the captivating world of Short Story Magic, your journey is an ongoing exploration of creativity, language mastery, and cultural connection. Crafting Narratives symbolizes the perpetual quest to harness the power of storytelling, communicate with eloquence, and create meaningful narratives that resonate with others.

By plunging into storytelling, you become a storyteller, a communicator, and a weaver of cultural threads. Each narrative you craft is an opportunity to learn, express, and connect with others through the universal language of stories.

As you tread upon your linguistic and imaginative pilgrimage, may each short story you create be a reminder of the limitless possibilities of language, a celebration of the art of storytelling, and a testament to the enduring magic of narratives in enriching our lives.

Cultivating Storytelling Proficiency

For a deeper layer of enrichment in your Short Story Magic experience and cultivate storytelling proficiency, consider these practical strategies:

1. Writing Challenges: Engage in writing challenges that prompt you to create short stories within specific themes or word limits. These challenges encourage you to think creatively and experiment with different narrative styles.

2. Story Circles: Form or join storytelling groups where members take turns contributing to a collective story. This collaborative exercise hones your improvisation skills and encourages dynamic storytelling.

3. Narrative Feedback: Share your stories with fellow learners or mentors to receive constructive feedback. Critiques and suggestions help you refine your narrative techniques and improve your writing.

4. Narrative Analysis: Study the works of renowned Chinese authors. Analyze their storytelling techniques, character development, and themes to gain insights into effective narrative construction.

Transferring Storytelling Knowledge Beyond Language

1. Narrative Presentations: Transform your stories into visual presentations. Create slideshows, animations, or short films that bring your narratives to life and engage multiple senses in the storytelling experience.

2. Community Storytelling: Organize storytelling events within your language learning community. Encourage participants to share their original stories, fostering a supportive and creative learning environment

Persistent Discovery of Storytelling Artistry

As you navigate the realm of Short Story Magic, always keep in mind that your path is a continuous voyage of imagination, expression, and connection. Crafting Narratives symbolizes the continuous quest to harness the magic of storytelling, nurture your creative voice, and foster meaningful connections through language.

By joining the ranks in storytelling, you not only create stories; you create bridges to cultures, emotions, and experiences. Each narrative you craft is a step towards developing your linguistic prowess, enhancing your communication skills, and leaving an indelible mark on the hearts of those who listen or read.

As you journey forth on your linguistic and creative migration, may each short story you pen be a reminder of the power of imagination, a celebration of the storyteller within you, and a testament to the enduring impact that narratives have in shaping our understanding of the world.

CHAPTER 17

Enchanted Escapade: The Enchanted Scroll - Dive into Mandarin through Story

Set foot on a magical journey into the heart of Enchanted Escapade, where language and storytelling intertwine to create an immersive adventure in Mandarin. In this chapter, we explore the captivating world of narrative language learning, delving into the concept of The Enchanted Scroll. Enchanted Escapade is more than a tale; it's a portal to linguistic exploration, cognitive engagement, and cultural discovery. Through this learning-oriented exploration, you'll uncover the art of learning through stories, master narrative language structures, and cultivate a deep connection with the Mandarin language. Get yourself set to unravel The

Enchanted Scroll and start off on a transformative language-learning experience.

The Essence of Enchanted Escapade: Beyond Words

1. Linguistic Engagement: Enchanted Escapade emphasizes that storytelling engages linguistic faculties, enhancing language comprehension and retention. By immersing yourself in stories, you activate your language skills and immerse in authentic contexts.

2. Cultural Voyage: Just as stories have cultural roots, they also provide a window into different worlds. By exploring The Enchanted Scroll, you gain insights into Mandarin linguistic nuances, idiomatic expressions, and cultural subtleties.

Unraveling The Enchanted Scroll: Language and Imagination

1. Narrative Structure: Engage in a deep exploration of the intricacies of narrative structure. Master phrases like **"从前有一位年轻人"** (**cóng qián yǒu yī wèi nián qīng rén**) - **"Once upon a time, there was a young person"** - to craft compelling story openings.

2. Dialogue Integration: Explore the art of integrating dialogue into narratives. Learn phrases like **"他说" (tā shuō) - "he said" - and "她问" (tā wèn) - "she asked" -** to bring characters to life and enhance storytelling dynamics.

3. Descriptive Language: Discover how to create vivid imagery through language. Master descriptive phrases like **"阳光照耀着大地" (yáng guāng zhào yào zhe dà dì) - "The sunlight illuminated the earth"** - to paint a vibrant picture for your readers.

Cultural Insights Through The Enchanted Scroll

1. Linguistic Nuances: Recognize linguistic nuances in narratives. Explore phrases like **"吉他的声音在空气中回荡" (jí tā de shēng yīn zài kōng qì zhōng huí dàng) - "The sound of the guitar echoed in the air"** - to understand the interplay between language and cultural context.

2. Cultural Expressions: Embrace idiomatic expressions and cultural references in narratives. Learn phrases like **"马到成功" (mǎ dào chéng gōng) - "success arrives immediately**

like a galloping horse" - to appreciate the cultural depth embedded in language.

The Enchanted Scroll in Action: Language Integration

1. Storytelling Challenges: Engage in storytelling challenges that encourage you to incorporate specific vocabulary or grammar structures into your narratives. These challenges enhance your language flexibility and creativity.

2. Narrative Retelling: Practice retelling existing stories in your own words. This exercise strengthens your language recall, comprehension, and ability to convey complex narratives.

Language Enhancement Through the Enchanted Scroll

1. Vocabulary Enrichment: Each narrative introduces new vocabulary. Explore the meanings and context of these words to expand your lexicon and enrich your narrative language.

2. Grammar Application: Analyze grammar structures within narratives. Understand sentence patterns **like "虽然**

...但是..." (suī rán... dàn shì...) - "although... but..." - to refine your grammatical accuracy and storytelling prowess.

The Enchanted Scroll in Action: Original Narratives

1. Personal Stories: Immerse yourself in crafting personal narratives. Develop stories based on your experiences, emotions, or imagination to practice narrative language structures.

2. Cultural Tales: Step into the world of Chinese culture by creating narratives that embody cultural elements, historical events, or societal dynamics. This exercise deepens your understanding of both language and culture.

Practical Application and Cultural Expression

1. Storytelling Performances: Share your stories through spoken performances or recordings. Practice oral fluency, pronunciation, and intonation while expressing your narratives.

2. Cultural Adaptation: Adapt traditional tales or folklore into Mandarin narratives. Retell stories like **"孙悟空" (sūn wù kōng) - "Monkey King"** - in your own words,

preserving cultural essence while enhancing your linguistic skills.

Learning Beyond the Enchanted Scroll: Imagination and Fluency

1. Literary Exploration: Explore a variety of Mandarin literature. Read narratives, short stories, and novels to expand your exposure to different narrative styles and language nuances.

2. Narrative Analysis: Engage in discussions about narrative techniques. Participate in conversations that dissect themes, character development, and cultural implications to deepen your narrative comprehension.

Continued Enchanted Escapade

As you navigate the enchanting realm of Enchanted Escapade, it's essential to bear in mind that your expedition is ongoing of creativity, language mastery, and cultural connection. The Enchanted Scroll symbolizes the continuous quest to dive into stories, refine your narrative prowess, and experience the transformative power of storytelling through language.

By affiliating with narrative language learning, you not only tell stories; you shape worlds, express emotions, and connect with the essence of Mandarin language and culture. Each narrative you craft becomes a testament to your linguistic journey, a vessel for cultural understanding, and a bridge that connects you with fellow storytellers across time and space.

Amidst your steady linguistic and narrative, may each story you create be a reminder of the boundless realms of imagination, a celebration of your unique narrative voice, and a testament to the enduring magic of storytelling in fostering language growth.

Cultivating Narrative Language Proficiency

To take your enrichment to the next level in Enchanted Escapade experience and cultivate narrative language proficiency, consider these practical strategies:

1. Narrative Workshops: Participate in narrative workshops that guide you through the process of crafting stories. Engage with prompts, exercises, and peer feedback to refine your narrative skills.

2. Collaborative Storytelling: Collaborate with fellow learners to create joint narratives. Each participant contributes a portion of the story, allowing you to practice cohesion, transition, and collective storytelling.

3. Narrative Analysis: Analyze well-known Mandarin stories. Deconstruct narratives to understand their structure, character development, and themes, enhancing your ability to create compelling tales.

4. Multimedia Narratives: Experiment with multimedia storytelling formats. Create illustrated narratives, audio recordings, or interactive digital stories to engage multiple senses and enhance your language learning experience.

Transferring Narrative Knowledge Beyond Storytelling

1. Cultural Showcases: Organize storytelling events that showcase narratives from different cultures. Share stories in Mandarin and encourage others to share tales from their own language backgrounds, promoting cross-cultural appreciation.

2. Narrative Presentations: Transform narratives into visual presentations. Develop slideshows, animations, or videos

that narrate your stories, enhancing your multimedia communication skills.

Continual Traverse of Narrative Mastery

During your search through the wondrous world of Enchanted Escapade, hold onto the fact that your passage is a constant unfolding of creativity, communication, and cultural immersion. The Enchanted Scroll represents the constant pursuit of narrative mastery, linguistic expression, and a deep connection with Mandarin storytelling.

By connecting oneself to narrative language learning, you become a storyteller, a communicator, and a language enthusiast. Each story you craft is an opportunity to probe intricately into the nuances of language, create meaningful connections, and inspire others through the beauty of narrative expression.

Through your continued linguistic and narrative passage, may each story you tell be a reminder of the limitless potential of language, a celebration of your storytelling artistry, and a testament to the enduring impact that narratives have on shaping our perceptions and connections with the world.

CHAPTER 18

Puzzle Pursuit: Mysteries Unveiled - Solving Puzzles in Mandarin

Welcome to the intriguing realm of Puzzle Pursuit, where language takes the form of enigmatic puzzles waiting to be deciphered. In this chapter, we commence a journey to an intellectual adventure through the world of language puzzles, exploring the art of problem-solving in Mandarin. Puzzle Pursuit is more than a mental challenge; it's a gateway to cognitive development, linguistic agility, and cultural insights. Through this learning-oriented exploration, you'll unlock the secrets of solving puzzles, master linguistic patterns, and cultivate a profound connection with the Mandarin language. Position yourself to unravel the mysteries and take the plunge into a transformative puzzle-solving journey.

The Essence of Puzzle Pursuit: Beyond Words

1. Cognitive Engagement: Puzzle Pursuit highlights that solving puzzles engages cognitive faculties, fostering critical thinking, and enhancing language processing skills. By immersing yourself in linguistic puzzles, you stimulate your mind and enhance your language proficiency.

2. Cultural Exploration: Just as puzzles are intricate, they also reveal cultural nuances. By delving into Puzzle Pursuit, you gain insights into Mandarin linguistic structures, idiomatic expressions, and cultural subtleties.

Unraveling Mysteries Unveiled: Language and Logic

1. Grammar Patterns: Probe intricately into the grammatical structures within puzzles. Master sentence patterns like **"是 ...的" (shì... de) - "It was... who..."** - to dissect and analyze linguistic constructions.

2. Vocabulary Inference: Explore the art of deducing vocabulary meanings from context. Learn how to use

phrases like **"根据上下文"** (**gēn jù shàng xià wén**) - **"based on context"** - to extract meaning from surrounding linguistic elements.

Cultural Insights Through Puzzle Pursuit

1. Linguistic Quirks: Recognize linguistic peculiarities embedded in puzzles. Explore phrases like **"一语双关"** (**yī yǔ shuāng guān**) - **"a pun in one sentence"** - to understand the role of wordplay in Mandarin language and culture.

2. Cultural Idioms: Embrace idiomatic expressions that hold cultural significance. Learn phrases like **"画蛇添足"** (**huà shé tiān zú**) - **"drawing legs on a snake"** - to appreciate the depth of cultural metaphors.

Puzzle Pursuit in Action: Language Integration

1. Puzzle Challenges: Engage in language puzzle challenges that require linguistic analysis and problem-solving. These challenges expand your language flexibility and analytical thinking.

2. Puzzle Workshops: Participate in puzzle-solving workshops that guide you through deciphering complex

linguistic constructs. Collaborate with peers to solve puzzles and share insights.

Language Enhancement Through Puzzle Pursuit

1. Vocabulary Enrichment: Each puzzle introduces new vocabulary. Explore the meanings and usage of these words to expand your lexicon and enhance your puzzle-solving capabilities.

2. Logical Reasoning: Analyze the logical flow of language in puzzles. Understand how phrases like **"如果...就..." (rú guǒ... jiù)** - **"if... then..."** - are used to convey conditional relationships.

Puzzle Pursuit in Action: Original Puzzles

1. Language Riddles: Craft linguistic riddles that challenge others to unravel. Develop puzzles that play with words, meanings, and cultural references to enhance your creativity and linguistic wit.

2. Cultural Enigmas: Design puzzles that incorporate cultural elements, historical references, or idiomatic expressions. This exercise deepens your understanding of both language and culture.

Practical Application and Analytical Skills

1. Puzzle Events: Organize puzzle-solving events within your language learning community. Collaborate with others to create and solve linguistic puzzles, fostering teamwork and analytical skills.

2. Translation Puzzles: Create puzzles that involve translating phrases from your native language to Mandarin. This exercise sharpens your translation abilities while enhancing your language comprehension.

Learning Beyond Puzzle Pursuit: Analytical Proficiency

1. Literary Exploration: Explore Mandarin literature for linguistic puzzles. Analyze poems, wordplay, and literary devices to deepen your understanding of linguistic creativity.

2. Analytical Discussions: Engage in discussions about linguistic nuances. Participate in conversations that dissect idioms, puns, and linguistic conundrums to refine your analytical and linguistic skills.

Continued Puzzle Mastery

As you move through the midst of the captivating world of Puzzle Pursuit, your journey is an ongoing exploration of logic, language, and cultural insight. Mysteries Unveiled symbolizes the perpetual quest to decode linguistic enigmas, refine your problem-solving prowess, and experience the transformative power of puzzles in language learning.

By becoming deeply involved in puzzle-solving, you become a linguistic detective, a critical thinker, and a master of linguistic manipulation. Each puzzle you solve becomes a testament to your linguistic journey, a testament to the intricate nature of language, and a key that unlocks the door to deeper cultural.

While you continue your path of understanding. Linguistic and analytical roaming, may each puzzle you decipher be a reminder of the limitless potential of language, a celebration of your problem-solving acumen, and a testament to the enduring fascination of puzzles in shaping our cognitive abilities.

Cultivating Puzzle-Solving Proficiency

To foster greater depth in your Puzzle Pursuit experience and cultivate puzzle-solving proficiency, consider these practical strategies:

1. Linguistic Brain Teasers: Engage in linguistic brain teasers and riddles. Challenge yourself with puzzles that require linguistic analysis, wordplay, and creative thinking to enhance your problem-solving skills.

2. Puzzle Collaboration: Collaborate with fellow language learners to solve puzzles. Work together to decipher complex linguistic constructs, sharing insights and learning from each other's approaches.

3. Puzzle Design: Design your own puzzles for others to solve. Craft linguistic challenges that test vocabulary, grammar, and cultural understanding, promoting active engagement and interactive learning.

4. Puzzle Apps and Games: Explore language puzzle apps and games. Use digital platforms to access a variety of puzzles that range from vocabulary crosswords to complex linguistic mysteries.

Transferring Puzzle Knowledge Beyond Language

1. Puzzle Events: Organize puzzle-solving events in your language learning community. Create puzzle challenges that encourage participants to use Mandarin to solve linguistic enigmas together.

2. Cultural Puzzles: Develop puzzles that revolve around cultural elements, historical events, or idiomatic expressions. This exercise deepens your connection with both language and culture.

Unceasing Roaming of Puzzle-Solving Mastery

During your travel through the intriguing world of Puzzle Pursuit, stay aware that your trek is an unending discovery of logic, language agility, and cultural insight. Mysteries Unveiled represents the constant pursuit of puzzle-solving mastery, cognitive dexterity, and a profound connection with the Mandarin language.

By participating eagerly in puzzle-solving, you not only decipher linguistic codes; you exercise your mind, refine your analytical skills, and uncover the hidden intricacies of language. Each puzzle you solve becomes a testament to your linguistic journey, a marker of your intellectual prowess, and a doorway to deeper linguistic understanding.

In your ongoing pursuit of linguistic and analytical sojourn, may each puzzle you conquer be a reminder of the boundless capacities of your mind, a celebration of your analytical creativity, and a testament to the enduring allure of puzzles in expanding our cognitive horizons.

CHAPTER 19

Expressions Explored: Emotion in Motion - Expressing Feelings in Mandarin

Step into the realm of emotional expression with Expressions Explored, where language becomes a conduit for the intricacies of human feelings. Within the confines of this chapter, we are to study the art of conveying emotions in Mandarin, exploring the depth and nuance of expressing feelings through language. Expressions Explored are more than just words; it's a gateway to empathy, communication, and cultural insights. Through this learning-oriented exploration, you'll unlock the power of emotional expression, master idiomatic phrases, and cultivate a profound connection with the Mandarin language. Get yourself ready to commence a trip of emotional discovery and linguistic mastery.

The Essence of Expressions Explored: Beyond Words

1. Emotional Engagement: Expressions Explored highlights that emotions are universal, transcending language barriers. By immersing yourself in emotional expressions, you enhance your empathy and connect deeply with Mandarin speakers.

2. Cultural Insight: Just as emotions are culturally influenced, they also reveal cultural nuances. By exploring Expressions Explored, you gain insights into Mandarin linguistic intricacies, idiomatic expressions, and cultural sensitivities.

Unraveling Emotion in Motion: Language and Empathy

1. Idiomatic Phrases: Look closely at the world of idiomatic expressions related to emotions. Master phrases like **"心情不好" (xīn qíng bù hǎo) - "in a bad mood"** - to convey emotions with depth and precision.

2. Tone and Intonation: Explore how tone and intonation convey different emotional nuances. Learn to modulate your

voice while using phrases like **"真的吗？"** (zhēn de ma?)

- **"Really?"** - to express curiosity or disbelief.

Cultural Insights Through Expressions Explored

1. Cultural Emotion Connotations: Recognize the cultural connotations of emotions. Explore phrases **like "大吃一惊" (dà chī yī jīng) - "to be greatly surprised"** - to understand how emotions are depicted in Mandarin culture.

2. Cultural Metaphors: Embrace emotional metaphors deeply embedded in the language. Learn phrases **like "一帆风顺" (yī fān fēng shùn) - "smooth sailing"** - to appreciate the cultural metaphors used to describe emotions.

Expression in Motion: Language Integration

1. Role-Play Activities: Engage in role-play scenarios to practice emotional expression. Embody different emotions while using phrases like **"我好高兴！"** (wǒ hǎo gāo xìng!)

- **"I'm so happy!"** - to refine your emotional communication skills.

2. Interactive Dialogues: Participate in interactive dialogues that focus on emotional exchanges. Engage in conversations where you express and respond to emotions, enhancing your real-life communication abilities.

Language Enhancement Through Expressions Explored

1. Vocabulary Expansion: Each emotional expression introduces new vocabulary. Explore the meanings and nuances of these words to enrich your emotional lexicon and convey emotions more effectively.

2. Contextual Usage: Analyze the context in which emotional expressions are used. Understand phrases like "我难过得不想吃东西" (wǒ nán guò de bù xiǎng chī dōng xi) - "I'm so upset that I don't want to eat" - to apply emotional expressions appropriately.

Expression in Motion: Personal Reflection

1. Emotional Journaling: Engage in emotional journaling in Mandarin. Write about your own emotions, experiences, and reflections, using a variety of emotional expressions to practice language use.

2. Cultural Comparisons: Compare emotional expressions in Mandarin with those in your native language. Analyze similarities and differences to deepen your cross-cultural understanding.

Practical Application and Interpersonal Skills

1. Emotional Conversations: Initiate conversations centered around emotions. Discuss personal experiences, opinions, and empathetic responses to emotional situations to enhance your interpersonal skills.

2. Empathetic Listening: Practice empathetic listening in Mandarin. Engage in conversations where you listen and respond to the emotions of others, cultivating your ability to connect on a deeper level.

Learning Beyond Emotional Expression: Connection and Communication

1. Literary Exploration: Explore Mandarin literature for emotional expression. Read poems, stories, and novels to grasp how emotions are intricately woven into linguistic and cultural contexts.

2. Cultural Discussions: Engage in discussions about cultural variations in emotional expression. Participate in conversations that explore how emotions are perceived and conveyed in different cultures.

Continued Expression Mastery

During your wayfaring through the realm of Expressions Explored, recollect that your sojourn is a never-ending quest of empathy, communication, and cultural understanding. Emotion in Motion represents the continuous quest to harness the power of emotional expression, connect with others on a profound level, and experience the transformative impact of emotions on language and culture.

By taking on the challenge of in emotional expression, you not only convey feelings; you build bridges of understanding, forge meaningful connections, and become a master of emotional communication. Each phrase you use becomes a testament to your linguistic journey, a vessel for heartfelt connection, and a bridge that spans across linguistic and cultural boundaries.

In the course of your linguistic and emotional venture, may each expression you employ be a reminder of the depth of human connection, a celebration of your empathetic communication, and a testament to the enduring resonance of emotions in shaping our relationships and linguistic interactions.

Cultivating Emotional Expression Proficiency

To intensify the richness of your Expressions Explored experience and cultivate emotional expression proficiency, consider these practical strategies:

1. Emotional Journaling: Dedicate a journal to recording your emotions in Mandarin. Write about daily experiences, events, and feelings using a variety of emotional expressions to enhance your language skills.

2. Conversational Scenarios: Create imaginary conversational scenarios where you express and respond to different emotions. Practice articulating your feelings authentically and sensitively.

3. Media Analysis: Analyze emotional expressions in Mandarin media. Watch movies, TV shows, or listen to music to identify how emotions are conveyed through dialogue, intonation, and body language.

4. Empathetic Listening Practice: Engage in listening exercises where you listen to authentic conversations in Mandarin and discern the emotional nuances in speakers' tones and expressions.

Transferring Emotional Expression Beyond Language

1. Cultural Exchange: Engage in language exchange with native Mandarin speakers. Share your emotional experiences and listen to theirs, fostering cross-cultural understanding and emotional empathy.

2. Creative Expression: Channel your emotions into creative outlets. Write poems, short stories, or create art that captures the essence of different emotions, allowing your linguistic and emotional expressions to intertwine.

Uninterrupted Sojourn of Emotional Connection

While you wend your way through the captivating world of Expressions Explored, your journey is an ongoing exploration of empathy, language mastery, and cultural insight. Emotion in Motion symbolizes the continuous pursuit of emotional connection, linguistic fluency, and a profound bond with the Mandarin language.

By becoming a participant in emotional expression, you become a bridge between languages, a cultivator of understanding, and a messenger of human experiences. Each emotion you convey becomes a testament to your linguistic journey, a vessel for authentic connection, and a thread that weaves together the tapestry of human emotions.

Throughout your unbroken linguistic and empathetic roving, may each expression you share be a reminder of the universal language of feelings, a celebration of your ability to connect deeply, and a testament to the enduring power of emotions in enriching our linguistic interactions and cultural appreciation.

CHAPTER 20

Traveler's Tales: Journey Chronicles - Travel Conversations in Mandarin

Start a new chapter in a linguistic voyage through Traveler's Tales, where language becomes a passport to exploration and cultural immersion. In this chapter, we venture into the world of travel conversations in Mandarin, unraveling the art of communication in various travel scenarios. Traveler's Tales is more than a guide; it's a gateway to cross-cultural connection, practical language application, and immersive experiences. Through this learning-oriented exploration, you'll uncover the intricacies of travel communication, master essential travel phrases, and cultivate a profound connection with the Mandarin language. Get yourself in gear to begin an expedition to a journey of global discovery and linguistic enrichment.

The Essence of Traveler's Tales: Beyond Words

1. Cultural Connection: Traveler's Tales highlights that travel conversations bridge cultures and foster understanding. By immersing yourself in travel dialogues, you connect authentically with locals and gain insights into diverse customs.

2. Practical Proficiency: Just as travel conversations are functional, they also reveal linguistic nuances. By exploring Traveler's Tales, you enhance your language fluency, situational adaptability, and real-life application.

Unraveling Journey Chronicles: Language and Exploration

1. Essential Phrases: Plunge into the essential travel phrases for various scenarios. Master expressions like **"请问这个地方怎么走?" (qǐng wèn zhè ge dì fāng zěn me zǒu?) -** **"Excuse me, how do I get to this place?"** - to navigate unfamiliar environments confidently.

2. Cultural Etiquette: Explore how cultural etiquette influences travel communication. Learn phrases like **"非常感谢您的帮助"** (**fēi cháng gǎn xiè nín de bāng zhù**) - **"Thank you very much for your help"** - to express gratitude respectfully.

Cultural Insights Through Traveler's Tales

1. Local Insights: Recognize the cultural insights embedded in travel conversations. Explore phrases like **"你喜欢这个城市吗?"** (**nǐ xǐ huān zhè ge chéng shì ma?**) - **"Do you like this city?"** - to initiate engaging discussions with locals.

2. Cultural Recommendations: Embrace phrases that facilitate cultural exchange. Learn expressions like **"您有什么好的推荐吗?"** (**nín yǒu shén me hǎo de tuī jiàn ma?**) - **"Do you have any good recommendations?"** - to discover local attractions and experiences.

Journey in Motion: Language Integration

1. Role-Play Scenarios: Engage in role-play exercises that simulate travel situations. Practice conversations where you

ask for directions, order food, or interact with locals, refining your communication skills.

2. Interactive Dialogues: Participate in interactive dialogues that mirror real travel encounters. Engage in conversations where you discuss travel plans, share experiences, and seek advice from others.

Language Enhancement Through Traveler's Tales

1. Vocabulary Expansion: Each travel scenario introduces new vocabulary. Explore the meanings and context of these words to enrich your travel-related lexicon and enhance your communication.

2. Situational Language: Analyze the situational language used in travel conversations. Understand phrases like **"我们需要两张去机场的票"** **(wǒmen xū yào liǎng zhāng qù jīchǎng de piào) - "We need two tickets to the airport"** - to apply travel phrases effectively

Journey in Motion: Personal Exploration

1. Travel Narratives: Craft imaginary travel narratives in Mandarin. Describe your travel experiences, encounters, and

adventures using a variety of travel-related expressions to enhance your language proficiency.

2. Cultural Comparisons: Compare travel customs and communication in Mandarin-speaking regions with those in your own culture. Analyze similarities and differences to deepen your cross-cultural understanding.

Practical Application and Intercultural Skills

1. Travel Conversations: Initiate conversations about travel experiences and plans. Share stories, discuss itineraries, and engage in travel-related discussions to enhance your practical language skills.

2. Cultural Exchange: Participate in cultural exchange activities while traveling. Interact with locals, share your experiences, and learn about their way of life to foster intercultural connection.

Learning Beyond Travel Conversations: Global Awareness

1. Literary Exploration: Explore travel literature in Mandarin. Read travelogues, articles, and blogs to gain

insights into how travel experiences are depicted and shared in the language.

2. Cultural Perspectives: Engage in discussions about cultural differences in travel communication. Participate in conversations that explore how communication styles and expectations vary across cultures.

Continued Journey Chronicles

As you maneuver through the captivating world of Traveler's Tales, let it sink in that your escapade is a constant quest for knowledge of cross-cultural connection, linguistic adaptability, and practical communication. Journey Chronicles symbolizes the continuous quest to harness the power of travel conversations, connect with diverse communities, and experience the transformative impact of language on global exploration.

By plunging into travel conversations, you not only communicate; you bridge cultures, foster understanding, and become a global citizen. Each dialogue you engage in becomes a testament to your linguistic journey, a key to unlocking cultural insights, and a door that opens to new horizons of connection.

While you advance on your linguistic and cultural jaunt, may each travel conversation you have be a reminder of the universal language of exploration, a celebration of your ability to connect authentically, and a testament to the enduring significance of communication in enriching our global perspectives and intercultural relationships.

Cultivating Travel Conversation Proficiency

To enrich your understanding and depth in Traveler's Tales experience and cultivate travel conversation proficiency, consider these practical strategies:

1. Language Exchange: Engage in language exchange with native Mandarin speakers who are passionate about travel. Share your travel experiences and learn about theirs, practicing travel conversations in an authentic context.

2. Role-Play Workshops: Participate in role-play workshops that simulate travel scenarios. Collaborate with fellow learners to practice ordering food, asking for directions, and sharing travel plans.

3. Travel Blogging: Start a travel blog or journal in Mandarin. Document your journeys, experiences, and

interactions in the language to enhance your travel-related vocabulary and expressions.

4. Travel Community Engagement: Join online travel communities or forums where Mandarin is spoken. Participate in discussions, share your insights, and learn from others' experiences to broaden your travel communication skills.

Transferring Travel Conversation Beyond Language

1. Cultural Exchange Events: Organize cultural exchange events where you and others share your travel experiences. Engage in cross-cultural discussions about travel customs, preferences, and communication styles.

2. Travel Presentations: Create presentations about your travel experiences in Mandarin. Share photos, anecdotes, and insights to enhance your presentation skills while practicing travel-related vocabulary.

Continuous Trek of Global Exploration

During your crossing of the captivating world of Traveler's Tales, your journey is an ongoing exploration of cultural immersion, linguistic versatility, and global awareness.

Journey Chronicles represents the continuous pursuit of travel conversation mastery, cross-cultural connection, and a profound bond with the Mandarin language.

By entering the sphere of travel conversations, you become a cultural ambassador, an open-minded traveler, and a bridge between languages. Each dialogue you initiate becomes a testament to your linguistic journey, a tool for authentic interaction, and a channel that connects you with fellow adventurers around the world.

Amid your determined linguistic and exploratory pioneering, may each travel conversation you embark upon be a reminder of the enriching possibilities of cross-cultural communication, a celebration of your ability to navigate diverse landscapes, and a testament to the enduring impact of language in shaping our global interactions and mutual understanding.

CHAPTER 21

Around the House: Home Portrayed - Describing Your Living Space

Step into the intimate realm of home and hearth with "Around the House," where language becomes a brush to paint vivid pictures of your living space. As we navigate through this chapter to examine the art of describing your home in Mandarin, unlocking the ability to convey the essence of your surroundings. "Around the House" is more than just a tour; it's a journey into self-expression, cultural representation, and linguistic immersion. Through this learning-oriented exploration, you'll uncover the nuances of describing living spaces, master spatial vocabulary, and cultivate a profound connection with the Mandarin language. Get into a state of readiness to open the doors to your home and share its essence with the world.

The Essence of "Around the House": Beyond Brick and Mortar

1. Personal Expression: "Around the House" highlights that describing your living space is a form of self-expression. By delving into the details of your home, you reveal facets of your identity and preferences.

2. Cultural Reflection: Just as homes are influenced by culture, they also serve as cultural mirrors. By exploring "Around the House," you gain insights into Mandarin linguistic structures, domestic customs, and cultural symbolism.

Unraveling Home Portrayed: Language and Ambiance

1. Spatial Vocabulary: Study meticulously into spatial vocabulary for different areas of your home. Master phrases like **"客厅" (kè tīng) - "living room"** - to accurately describe various spaces and their functions.

2. Adjectives and Nuances: Explore adjectives that capture the ambiance of your home. Learn words like **"舒适" (shū**

shì) - "comfortable" - to convey the feeling you wish to evoke.

Cultural Insights Through "Around the House"

1. Cultural Influences: Recognize cultural influences on home description. Explore phrases like **"餐桌上有一个红色的花瓶" (cān zhuō shàng yǒu yī ge hóng sè de huā píng) - "There is a red vase on the dining table"** - to understand how cultural aesthetics shape descriptions.

2. Symbolic Imagery: Embrace phrases that carry symbolic imagery. Learn expressions like **"书架上摆满了书" (shū jià shàng bǎi mǎn le shū) - "The bookshelf is filled with books"** - to appreciate the cultural value of knowledge.

Home in Motion: Language Integration

1. Descriptive Dialogues: Engage in descriptive dialogue exercises. Practice conversations where you describe your home, discuss interior design, and share your preferences, enhancing your descriptive skills.

2. Virtual Tours: Participate in virtual home tours with fellow learners. Describe each other's living spaces, fostering interactivity and collaborative language learning.

Language Enhancement Through "Around the House"

1. Vocabulary Enrichment: Each room description introduces new vocabulary. Explore the meanings and usage of these words to enrich your home-related lexicon and elevate your descriptions.

2. Descriptive Fluency: Analyze the structure of descriptive sentences. Understand phrases like **"我家的厨房非常宽敞明亮"** **(wǒ jiā de chú fáng fēi cháng kuān zhǎng míng liàng)** - "The kitchen in my home is very spacious and bright" - to apply descriptive language effectively.

Home in Motion: Personal Imagination

1. Home Narratives: Craft imaginative narratives about your living space in Mandarin. Describe the atmosphere, layout, and personal touches to enhance your language proficiency.

2. Cultural Comparisons: Compare home design and functionality in Mandarin-speaking regions with those in

your own culture. Analyze similarities and differences to deepen your cross-cultural understanding.

Practical Application and Descriptive Skills

1. Home Conversations: Initiate conversations about homes and living spaces. Discuss décor, furniture, and arrangements to practice descriptive language in real-life scenarios.

2. Cultural Exchange: Share your home description with Mandarin speakers. Invite them to describe their homes, creating a cross-cultural dialogue and fostering intercultural connection.

Learning Beyond Home Portrayal: Cultural Interpretation

1. Literary Exploration: Explore literature that features home descriptions. Read novels, short stories, and essays to understand how living spaces are depicted in Mandarin literature.

2. Cultural Discussions: Engage in discussions about cultural symbolism in home design. Participate in

conversations that explore how homes reflect values, social norms, and individual identities.

Continued Home Portrayal

As you explore through the intimate world of "Around the House," embrace the concept that your expedition is a perpetual unfolding of self-expression, cultural insight, and linguistic creativity. Home Portrayed symbolizes the continuous quest to convey the essence of your living space, connect with others through descriptive language, and experience the transformative power of words in shaping our perceptions of home.

By embracing wholeheartedly in home portrayal, you not only describe a physical space; you evoke emotions, share stories, and become a storyteller of the spaces you inhabit. Each description you create becomes a testament to your linguistic journey, a window into your world, and a doorway to deeper cultural understanding.

During your unrelenting linguistic and imaginative adventure, may each portrayal of your home be a reminder of the beauty of self-expression, a celebration of your descriptive artistry, and a testament to the enduring resonance of language in shaping our perceptions of the spaces we inhabit.

Cultivating Descriptive Proficiency

To immerse yourself further in the enrichment of your "Around the House" experience and cultivate descriptive proficiency, consider these practical strategies:

1. Home Tour Practice: Take virtual or in-person home tours and describe what you see in Mandarin. Practice your descriptive skills by narrating the layout, décor, and features of different spaces.

2. Comparative Analysis: Compare home descriptions in Mandarin with those in your native language. Identify cultural variations in how homes are portrayed and expand your descriptive vocabulary.

3. Creative Writing: Engage in creative writing exercises to describe your dream home or an imaginary living space. Challenge yourself to use vivid adjectives and evoke emotions through your descriptions.

4. Collaborative Descriptions: Collaborate with language partners to describe each other's homes. Provide feedback on

each other's descriptions to enhance your descriptive language use.

Transferring Home Portrayal Beyond Language

1. Home Sharing Events: Organize home-sharing events where participants describe their homes in Mandarin. Exchange ideas, share design tips, and celebrate the diversity of living spaces.

2. Cultural Immersion: Immerse yourself in Mandarin-speaking home décor and architecture media. Watch home improvement shows, read design magazines, and explore online platforms to learn about cultural influences on home portrayal.

Undying Expedition of Descriptive Creativity

During your trek across the intimate world of "Around the House," reaffirm the notion that your voyage is a lifetime of exploration of creativity, self-representation, and cross-cultural appreciation. Home Portrayed represents the continuous pursuit of descriptive mastery, cultural interpretation, and a profound bond with the Mandarin language.

By devoting oneself in home portrayal, you become an artist of words, a connoisseur of ambiance, and a bridge between languages and cultures. Each description you craft becomes a testament to your linguistic journey, a testament to your storytelling prowess, and a canvas that captures the essence of your living space.

In your ongoing linguistic and creative itinerary, may each portrayal of your home be a reminder of the beauty of descriptive language, a celebration of your unique perspective, and a testament to the enduring impact of words in shaping our understanding of the spaces we inhabit.

CHAPTER 22

Accent Artistry: Accent Transformation - Perfecting Mandarin Pronunciation

Step onto the stage of linguistic finesse with "Accent Artistry," where language becomes a symphony of sounds waiting to be perfected. Amidst this chapter's content, we will study deeply into the art of accent transformation in Mandarin, unlocking the keys to achieving impeccable pronunciation. "Accent Artistry" is more than just a lesson; it's a voyage into vocal mastery, cultural immersion, and linguistic fluency. Through this learning-oriented exploration, you'll uncover the intricacies of accent adjustment, master tone modulation, and cultivate a profound connection with the Mandarin language. Ready up yourself to fine-tune your speech and launch into a journey of auditory excellence.

The Essence of "Accent Artistry": Beyond Words and Sounds

1. Personal Connection: "Accent Artistry" highlights that mastering pronunciation is a personal journey. By refining your accent, you connect more deeply with native speakers and increase your linguistic confidence.

2. Cultural Adaptation: Just as accents reflect cultural influences, they also serve as cultural bridges. By exploring "Accent Artistry," you gain insights into Mandarin linguistic nuances, tonal patterns, and social interactions.

Unraveling Accent Transformation: Language and Harmony

1. Tonal Precision: Delve deeply into tonal precision for Mandarin syllables. Master tones like **"一" (yī) - "one"** - to produce accurate intonation and convey meaning without ambiguity.

2. Phonetic Challenges: Explore common phonetic challenges for non-native speakers. Learn to distinguish between similar sounds, such as **"sh" and "s,"** to enhance your overall clarity.

Cultural Insights Through "Accent Artistry"

1. Cultural Connotations: Recognize the cultural connotations of different accents. Explore how pronunciation can influence social perceptions and interactions within Mandarin-speaking communities.

2. Accent Variations: Embrace accent variations across Mandarin-speaking regions. Learn about differences in pronunciation and how they reflect regional identity and linguistic diversity.

Accent in Motion: Language Integration

1. Dialogue Exercises: Engage in dialogue exercises that focus on accent adjustment. Practice conversations where you emulate native pronunciation, refining your auditory accuracy.

2. Mimicry and Repetition: Participate in mimicry and repetition drills. Listen to native speakers and imitate their pronunciation, honing your accent transformation skills.

Language Enhancement Through "Accent Artistry"

1. Vocabulary Integration: Each pronunciation exercise introduces new vocabulary. Explore the meanings and usage

of these words to expand your lexicon while perfecting your pronunciation.

2. Contextual Pronunciation: Analyze the context in which specific sounds are pronounced. Understand how phrases like **"我要去商店买东西"** (**wǒ yào qù shāng diàn mǎi dōng xi**) - **"I want to go to the store to buy things"** - impact accent and tone.

Accent in Motion: Personal Progress

1. Record and Compare: Record your speech and compare it with native speakers. Identify areas for improvement and work on refining your accent based on feedback.

2. Cultural Comparisons: Compare accents across different Mandarin-speaking regions. Analyze similarities and differences to gain a deeper understanding of how accents reflect cultural and linguistic nuances.

Practical Application and Auditory Skills

1. Accent Adjustment Conversations: Engage in conversations focused on accent transformation. Discuss pronunciation challenges, share tips, and practice adjusting your accent in real-life interactions.

2. Accent Exchange: Pair up with native speakers for accent exchange sessions. Help each other refine accents in both Mandarin and your native language, fostering mutual language improvement.

Learning Beyond Accent Transformation: Cross-Cultural Adaptation

1. Media Exploration: Listen to podcasts, watch movies, and engage with Mandarin media to immerse yourself in native accents. Familiarize yourself with different accents to enhance your listening skills.

2. Cultural Discussions: Engage in discussions about accents and communication. Participate in conversations that explore how accents influence social dynamics, linguistic perceptions, and cultural adaptation

Continued Accent Artistry

While you move through the melodious world of "Accent Artistry," reflect upon the idea that your adventure is a continuous unfolding of auditory refinement, cross-cultural adaptation, and linguistic artistry. Accent Transformation symbolizes the continuous quest to harmonize your speech, connect authentically with native speakers, and experience the transformative impact of impeccable pronunciation.

By becoming engrossed in accent transformation, you not only adjust your speech; you bridge linguistic gaps, communicate with clarity, and become a harmonious participant in Mandarin conversations. Each sound you articulate becomes a testament to your linguistic journey, a note in the symphony of communication, and an instrument that resonates with cultural and linguistic nuances.

As you maintain your linguistic and auditory progress, may each accent transformation you undertake be a reminder of the power of sound, a celebration of your dedication to linguistic accuracy, and a testament to the enduring significance of pronunciation in shaping our connections and interactions.

Cultivating Accent Transformation Proficiency

To deepen your connection and enrichment in "Accent Artistry" experience and cultivate accent transformation proficiency, consider these practical strategies:

1. Shadowing Exercises: Engage in shadowing exercises where you listen to native speakers and repeat their

sentences in real time. Focus on mimicking their pronunciation, intonation, and rhythm.

2. Pronunciation Apps: Utilize language learning apps that provide pronunciation feedback. These apps often use speech recognition technology to help you identify and correct pronunciation errors.

3. Language Partners: Practice accent transformation with language partners who are native Mandarin speakers. Regular conversations and feedback sessions will help you refine your accent.

4. Phonetic Practice: Explore phonetic exercises that focus on specific sound pairs or groups. Practice minimal pairs and tongue twisters to improve your articulation and accuracy.

Transferring Accent Transformation Beyond Language

1. Media Immersion: Immerse yourself in authentic Mandarin media. Listen to radio shows, podcasts, and news broadcasts to expose yourself to various accents and enhance your listening skills.

2. Language Exchange Events: Participate in language exchange events where native speakers of Mandarin and

your native language come together to practice speaking and improve accents.

Limitless Adventure of Vocal Elegance

As you traverse the harmonious world of "Accent Artistry," never lose sight of the fact that your path is an eternal exploration of auditory finesse, cultural adaptability, and linguistic dexterity. Accent Transformation represents the continuous pursuit of accent mastery, effective communication, and a profound bond with the Mandarin language.

By delving into in accent transformation, you become a conductor of pronunciation, a performer of linguistic melodies, and a bridge between languages and cultures. Each sound you refine becomes a testament to your linguistic journey, a thread in the tapestry of communication, and a note that resonates with the beauty of cross-cultural exchange.

While you progress in your linguistic and auditory safari, may each accent transformation you embark upon be a reminder of the elegance of sound, a celebration of your commitment to sonic precision, and a testament to the enduring impact of pronunciation in enriching our linguistic interactions and cross-cultural connections.

CHAPTER 23

Language Hurdles and Triumphs: Tackling Tones - Conquering the Tone Challenge

Set out on a quest for a journey of linguistic triumphs and overcome challenges with "Language Hurdles and Triumphs." In this segment, we explore into the intricacies of mastering Mandarin tones, unraveling the enigma of tonal pronunciation. "Tackling Tones" is more than a lesson; it's a path to tonal mastery, cultural insight, and linguistic resilience. Through this learning-oriented exploration, you'll uncover the complexities of Mandarin tones, develop strategies to conquer them, and cultivate a profound connection with the Mandarin language. Prime yourself to conquer the tone challenge and embrace the thrill of linguistic triumph.

The Essence of "Language Hurdles and Triumphs": The Tonal Quest

1. Personal Empowerment: "Language Hurdles and Triumphs" highlights that conquering tones empowers you to communicate confidently. By overcoming tonal challenges, you strengthen your language foundation and boost your linguistic self-assurance.

2. Cultural Bridge: Just as tones shape communication, they also bridge cultures. By exploring "Language Hurdles and Triumphs," you gain insights into Mandarin phonology, social interactions, and regional diversity.

Unraveling Tackling Tones: Sound and Resilience

1. Tonal Identification: Investigate profoundly into the identification of Mandarin tones. Master recognizing and producing the four tones - first, second, third, and fourth - to communicate with precision.

2. Tonal Contours: Explore tonal contours and their impact on meaning. Understand how changing tones can alter the

semantics of a word, as seen in "ma" with different tones signifying different meanings.

Cultural Insights Through "Language Hurdles and Triumphs"

1. Tonal Nuances: Recognize the cultural nuances conveyed through tones. Explore how tonal inflections influence emotional expression and convey subtle shades of meaning.

2. Dialectal Variations: Embrace dialectal variations in tones. Learn about how different Mandarin-speaking regions may exhibit distinct tonal patterns, reflecting their unique linguistic identities.

Tone in Action: Language Integration

1. Tone Practice Dialogues: Engage in dialogue exercises that focus on mastering tones. Practice conversations where you emphasize correct tonal pronunciation, refining your communication skills.

2. Tone Drills: Participate in tone drills that challenge your tonal accuracy. Use audio resources and mimic native speakers to improve your tone production.

Language Enhancement Through "Language Hurdles and Triumphs"

1. Tone Vocabulary: Each tone practice introduces new vocabulary. Explore the meanings and context of these words to enrich your tonal lexicon while refining your pronunciation.

2. Tone Application: Analyze the application of tones in sentences. Understand how tones interact with each other and influence the overall melody of Mandarin speech.

Tone in Action: Personal Persistence

1. Regular Practice: Devote time to regular tone practice. Incorporate tonal exercises into your daily routine to develop muscle memory and improve your tonal accuracy.

2. Tone Mimicry: Listen to native speakers and mimic their tonal patterns. Focus on emulating their tones and rhythm to enhance your overall tonal fluency.

Practical Application and Tonal Skills

1. Tone Accuracy Conversations: Engage in conversations focused on tonal accuracy. Discuss tonal challenges, share

tips, and practice producing accurate tones in real-life interactions.

2. Tonal Exchange: Collaborate with language partners to practice tonal accuracy. Correct each other's tones in both structured exercises and spontaneous conversations.

Learning Beyond Tonal Triumphs: Cross-Linguistic Skills

1. Multilingual Exploration: Compare tones in Mandarin with those in other tonal languages. Explore similarities and differences in tonal systems to deepen your understanding of linguistic diversity.

2. Cultural Discussions: Engage in discussions about tonal perception and social dynamics. Participate in conversations that explore how tones influence linguistic perceptions and interpersonal interactions

Continued Tonal Mastery

While maneuvering the challenging yet rewarding world of "Language Hurdles and Triumphs," continuously remind yourself that your journey is a boundless voyage of resilience, linguistic precision, and cultural connection.

Tackling Tones symbolizes the continuous quest to conquer tonal intricacies, communicate effectively, and experience the transformative power of mastering tones.

By involving oneself in tonal mastery, you become a virtuoso of pronunciation, a conductor of linguistic melody, and a bridge between languages and cultures. Each tone you conquer becomes a testament to your linguistic journey, a musical note in the symphony of speech, and a building block in your path towards Mandarin fluency.

While you march on with your linguistic and tonal march, may each tonal triumph you achieve be a reminder of the beauty of linguistic diversity, a celebration of your perseverance in mastering tones, and a testament to the enduring significance of pronunciation in shaping our communicative interactions and cross-cultural connections.

Cultivating Tonal Mastery

To cultivate greater richness in your "Language Hurdles and Triumphs" experience and cultivate tonal mastery, consider these practical strategies:

1. Daily Tonal Exercises: Incorporate daily tonal exercises into your language learning routine. Practice tone drills,

repeat tonal patterns, and engage in focused exercises to strengthen your tonal accuracy.

2. Tonal Analysis: Analyze tonal patterns in different contexts. Listen to various Mandarin resources, such as songs, podcasts, and news broadcasts, to identify tonal variations in real-life speech.

3. Tone-Color Associations: Develop associations between tones and colors to enhance your memory of tonal distinctions. Assign a specific color to each tone to reinforce your ability to differentiate them.

4. Visual Aids: Use visual aids like tone charts and diagrams to visualize the trajectory of each tone. Incorporate these aids into your practice sessions to reinforce tonal memory.

Transferring Tonal Mastery Beyond Language

1. Song Singing: Sing Mandarin songs that emphasize tonal variations. Singing helps you internalize tonal patterns and melodies, enhancing your overall tonal accuracy.

2. Storytelling Practice: Narrate stories in Mandarin, focusing on maintaining accurate tones. Engage in creative storytelling exercises to strengthen your tonal fluency.

Unfaltering Exploration of Tonal Proficiency

While progressing through the intricate world of "Language Hurdles and Triumphs," keep the thought alive that your travels are an ongoing revelation of linguistic precision, cultural adaptation, and auditory skill. Tackling Tones represents the continuous pursuit of tonal mastery, effective communication, and a profound bond with the Mandarin language.

By absorbing oneself in tonal conquest, you become a maestro of intonation, a linguist of sonic subtleties, and a bridge between languages and cultures. Each tone you conquer becomes a testament to your linguistic journey, a musical note that harmonizes cross-cultural connections, and a testament to the enduring resonance of tones in shaping our linguistic interactions.

During your unwavering resolve to linguistic and tonal ramble, may each tone you tackle be a reminder of the beauty of auditory diversity, a celebration of your determination in mastering tonal intricacies, and a testament to the enduring impact of pronunciation in enriching our linguistic connections and global understanding.

CHAPTER 24

Character Chronicles: Characters in Context - Navigating Chinese Characters

ake the first strides towards a fascinating expedition into the world of Chinese characters with "Character Chronicles." As we proceed in this chapter, dive into the intricate art of navigating and understanding Chinese characters, unlocking the keys to deciphering the written language. "Characters in Context" is more than a lesson; it's a voyage into visual symbolism, cultural insight, and linguistic exploration. Through this learning-oriented exploration, you'll unravel the mysteries of Chinese characters, develop strategies for character recognition, and cultivate a profound connection with the

Mandarin language. Be prepared to launch into a new experience of visual literacy and discover the beauty within the strokes.

The Essence of "Character Chronicles": Beyond Symbols and Strokes

1. Visual Literacy: "Character Chronicles" emphasizes that understanding characters fosters visual literacy. By exploring the intricacies of characters, you become adept at decoding visual symbols and grasping their meanings.

2. Cultural Insights: Just as characters embody culture, they also reflect historical and societal contexts. By delving into "Character Chronicles," you gain insights into Mandarin linguistics, cultural symbolism, and the evolution of written communication.

Unraveling Characters in Context: Meaning and Composition

1. Character Components: Scrutinize closely into the composition of Chinese characters. Learn about radicals, phonetics, and semantic components that combine to form characters and convey meanings.

2. Stroke Order: Explore the importance of stroke order in character writing. Understand how correct stroke sequences enhance character recognition and writing fluency.

Cultural Insights Through "Character Chronicles"

1. Symbolic Significance: Recognize the symbolic significance of characters. Explore how characters like **"福"** **(fú) - "fortune"** - embody cultural values and hold auspicious meanings in various contexts.

2. Historical Evolution: Embrace characters' historical evolution. Learn about simplified and traditional characters, and understand their roles in modern communication and cultural preservation.

Characters in Action: Language Integration

1. Character Practice: Engage in character recognition exercises. Practice identifying characters, understanding their meanings, and differentiating between similar-looking characters.

2. Character Writing: Participate in character writing sessions. Practice correct stroke order and character composition to enhance your character-writing skills.

Language Enhancement Through "Character Chronicles"

1. Vocabulary Expansion: Each character introduces new vocabulary. Explore the meanings and applications of characters to enrich your lexicon while deepening your understanding of their usage.

2. Contextual Interpretation: Analyze characters in context. Understand how characters combine to form words and phrases, allowing you to decipher meaning within a sentence.

Characters in Action: Personal Exploration

1. Character Analysis: Select characters and analyze their components. Break down characters into radicals, phonetics, and semantics to grasp their meanings and build a foundation for character recognition.

2. Character Mnemonics: Develop mnemonic techniques to remember characters. Create associations between characters and their meanings to aid in character retention.

Practical Application and Character Proficiency

1. Character Conversation: Engage in conversations centered around characters. Discuss character meanings, etymology, and cultural implications to strengthen your character knowledge.

2. Character Exchange: Collaborate with language partners to exchange characters. Share characters that are challenging or interesting, and help each other understand their meanings and usage.

Learning Beyond Character Chronicles: Cultural Appreciation

1. Literary Exploration: Explore literature featuring character analysis. Read texts that analyze thoroughly into characters' symbolism, historical context, and cultural connotations to deepen your appreciation.

2. Cultural Discussions: Engage in discussions about characters' role in cultural expression. Participate in conversations that explore how characters shape written communication and cultural identity.

Continued Character Navigations

In the act of navigating the intricate world of "Character Chronicles," hold onto the understanding that your adventure is a continuous unveiling of visual comprehension, cultural immersion, and linguistic insight. Characters in Context represents the continuous quest to decipher characters, connect with the written language, and experience the transformative power of visual literacy.

By getting involved in character navigation, you become an interpreter of symbols, a curator of linguistic history, and a bridge between visual and spoken languages. Each character you decipher becomes a testament to your linguistic journey, a brushstroke in the canvas of communication, and a key that unlocks the door to cross-cultural understanding.

Amid your persistent linguistic and visual wayfaring, may each character you navigate be a reminder of the beauty of visual language, a celebration of your dedication to character comprehension, and a testament to the enduring impact of written symbols in shaping our written and spoken interactions.

Cultivating Character Navigation Proficiency

To heighten your immersion and enrichment in "Character Chronicles" experience and cultivate character navigation proficiency, consider these practical strategies:

1. Character Flashcards: Create flashcards with characters on one side and their meanings and pronunciations on the other. Review these flashcards regularly to reinforce your character recognition skills.

2. Character Etymology: Dive deeper into character etymology. Explore the historical origins of characters, their evolution, and the stories behind their formation to gain a deeper understanding.

3. Language Partnerships: Collaborate with language partners to practice character recognition and writing. Test each other's knowledge, share character insights, and engage in character-focused conversations.

4. Contextual Reading: Read Chinese texts, such as news articles, short stories, and online forums, to see characters in context. Pay attention to how characters contribute to the overall meaning of the text.

Transferring Character Navigation Beyond Language

1. Character Art: Explore calligraphy and character art as a form of creative expression. Practice writing characters in different styles and sizes, combining linguistic and artistic skills.

2. Historical Exploration: Study ancient texts and inscriptions to observe how characters have evolved over time. Analyze historical artifacts to deepen your understanding of character usage.

Ageless Wander of Character Comprehension

Throughout your exploration of the intricate world of "Character Chronicles," allow yourself to realize that your expedition is a perpetual discovery of visual acuity, cultural appreciation, and linguistic exploration. Characters in Context represents the continuous quest to unravel characters' meanings, engage with the written word, and experience the transformative power of visual literacy.

By engaging in character navigation, you become a connoisseur of symbols, a curator of linguistic heritage, and a bridge between visual and spoken forms of communication. Each character you decipher becomes a testament to your linguistic journey, a brushstroke in the tapestry of written expression, and a symbol that unites cultures and languages.

During your unrelenting devotion to linguistic and visual roving, may each character you navigate be a reminder of the elegance of visual language, a celebration of your commitment to character comprehension, and a testament to the enduring impact of written symbols in shaping our understanding of language, culture, and human expression.

CHAPTER 25

Time Traveler's Guide: Temporal Talk - Navigating Verb Tenses in Mandarin

Embark upon a new phase of a captivating journey through time with the "Time Traveler's Guide." Within this part, we uncover the intricate world of verb tenses in Mandarin, unveiling the secrets to expressing time and actions with precision. "Temporal Talk" is not just a lesson; it's a voyage into linguistic chronology, cultural context, and grammatical finesse. Through this learning-oriented exploration, you'll unravel the complexities of Mandarin verb tenses, develop strategies to navigate them effectively, and cultivate a profound connection with the Mandarin language. Make preparations to initiate an exploration of a journey through time and master the art of temporal expression.

The Essence of "Time Traveler's Guide": Beyond Past, Present, and Future

1. Temporal Precision: "Time Traveler's Guide" emphasizes that mastering verb tenses allows you to convey actions in precise temporal contexts. By delving into verb tenses, you enhance your ability to express actions with accuracy.

2. Cultural Insight: Just as verb tenses reflect temporal nuances, they also mirror cultural perspectives on time. Exploring "Temporal Talk" provides insights into Mandarin linguistics, cultural interpretations, and historical contexts.

Unraveling Temporal Talk: Grammar and Context

1. Tense Variations: Search deeply into the various verb tenses in Mandarin, including past, present, future, and continuous tenses. Understand how each tense conveys specific temporal information.

2. Temporal Markers: Explore temporal markers that signal different tenses. Learn how words like "了" (le), "在" (zài), and "将" (jiāng) contribute to temporal clarity in sentences.

Cultural Insights Through "Time Traveler's Guide"

1. Cultural Temporal Conceptions: Recognize how different cultures perceive and express time. Compare Mandarin temporal expressions with those in your native language to gain cross-cultural insights.

2. Historical Temporal Context: Embrace the historical context that influences temporal expressions. Learn how cultural and historical events shape the way time is conceptualized and communicated.

Temporal Talk in Action: Language Integration

1. Temporal Practice Dialogues: Engage in dialogue exercises that focus on various verb tenses. Practice crafting sentences that accurately express actions in different temporal contexts.

2. Temporal Sentence Construction: Participate in sentence construction drills. Create sentences that incorporate specific verb tenses to reinforce your temporal grammar skills.

Language Enhancement Through "Time Traveler's Guide"

1. Vocabulary Expansion: Each temporal exercise introduces new vocabulary. Explore the meanings and applications of

these words to expand your lexicon while refining your grasp of temporal expressions.

2. Contextual Interpretation: Analyze sentences in context to understand how verb tenses influence the overall meaning. Explore how tense choices impact the narrative of a sentence.

Temporal Talk in Action: Personal Application

1. Temporal Storytelling: Craft short narratives that use various verb tenses. Tell stories that involve different temporal contexts to practice applying tense knowledge in practical scenarios.

2. Temporal Journaling: Keep a journal where you describe daily activities using different verb tenses. Document your experiences in past, present, and future tenses to reinforce temporal accuracy.

Practical Application and Temporal Mastery

1. Temporal Conversation: Engage in conversations centered around temporal expressions. Discuss cultural perceptions of time, share insights on tense usage, and practice crafting sentences.

2. Temporal Exchange: Collaborate with language partners to exchange sentences in different verb tenses. Provide feedback and insights on each other's tense usage to enhance temporal mastery.

Learning Beyond "Time Traveler's Guide": Cultural Awareness

1. Media Exploration: Watch movies, listen to songs, and engage with Mandarin media to observe how different verb tenses are used in natural language and cultural contexts.

2. Cultural Discussions: Engage in conversations about cultural interpretations of time. Explore how verb tenses shape narratives, influence communication, and reflect cultural attitudes.

Continued Temporal Mastery

As you navigate the intricate world of the "Time Traveler's Guide," stay mindful of the fact that your passage is an unending quest of temporal precision, cultural resonance, and grammatical proficiency. Temporal Talk represents the continuous quest to master verb tenses, convey actions in accurate time frames, and experience the transformative power of temporal expression.

By immersing oneself temporal mastery, you become a navigator of linguistic chronology, a weaver of temporal narratives, and a bridge between past, present, and future linguistic contexts. Each sentence you construct becomes a testament to your linguistic journey, a marker in the tapestry of time, and a key that unlocks the door to cross-cultural understanding.

As you keep pushing on your linguistic and temporal outing, may each tense you master be a reminder of the elegance of temporal language, a celebration of your dedication to grammatical accuracy, and a testament to the enduring impact of tense usage in shaping our narrative expressions and intercultural connections.

Cultivating Temporal Mastery

To further enrich your "Time Traveler's Guide" experience and cultivate temporal mastery, consider these practical strategies:

1. Daily Temporal Journal: Keep a daily journal where you describe your activities using different verb tenses. This practice helps reinforce your understanding of tense usage in practical scenarios.

2. Temporal Storytelling: Practice telling stories using various verb tenses. Create narratives that involve different time frames to develop your ability to switch between tenses fluently.

3. Tense Switching Games: Play language games with friends or language partners where you switch between verb tenses while conversing. This dynamic exercise hones your ability to apply tenses spontaneously.

4. Temporal Reading: Read texts in Mandarin that involve different verb tenses. Analyze how authors use tenses to create a sense of time and context within their narratives.

Transferring Temporal Mastery Beyond Language

1. Historical Exploration: Study historical events or periods and discuss them using different verb tenses. Engage in conversations or write essays to describe past occurrences in accurate temporal frames.

2. Temporal Art: Create art that reflects different time frames. Paint or illustrate scenes from the past, present, and future to visually represent temporal concepts.

Endless Jaunt of Temporal Proficiency

In the midst of navigating the intricate world of the "Time Traveler's Guide," don't forget that your path is an ongoing quest for self-discovery of grammatical precision, cultural understanding, and linguistic versatility. Temporal Talk represents the continuous pursuit of mastering verb tenses, communicating with temporal accuracy, and experiencing the transformative power of temporal expression.

By becoming a participant in temporal navigation, you become a steward of linguistic chronicles, a conductor of narrative time, and a bridge between temporal dimensions. Each tense you master becomes a testament to your linguistic journey, a marker that weaves the fabric of time, and a guide that navigates the intricacies of intercultural and interpersonal communication.

Throughout your unfaltering linguistic and temporal flight, may each tense you conquer be a reminder of the beauty of temporal language, a celebration of your commitment to grammatical fluency, and a testament to the enduring impact of tense usage in shaping our understanding of time, communication, and cultural connections.

CHAPTER 26

Music and Language: Harmonious Learning - Enhancing with Mandarin Music

Initiate a quest to a melodious exploration of language and music with "Music and Language." Here, we dig deeper into the powerful synergy between Mandarin language learning and music, discovering how harmonious melodies can amplify your linguistic journey. "Harmonious Learning" is not just a lesson; it's a symphony of auditory immersion, cultural connection, and cognitive enhancement. Through this learning-oriented exploration, you'll unravel the connection between music and language, develop strategies for integrating Mandarin music into your studies, and cultivate a profound connection with the Mandarin language. Get in position to harmonize your learning experience and let the rhythms guide your linguistic progress.

The Essence of "Music and Language": Where Sound Meets Expression

1. Auditory Sensitivity: "Music and Language" underscores how music sharpens your auditory sensitivity. By exploring the relationship between music and language, you enhance your ability to perceive and reproduce sounds accurately.

2. Cultural Resonance: Just as music resonates with cultural nuances, it also echoes through language. By delving into "Harmonious Learning," you gain insights into the melodic soul of Mandarin, cultural contexts, and the fusion of artistic expression.

Unraveling Harmonious Learning: The Language-Music Connection

1. Rhythmic Patterns: Explore the rhythmic patterns shared between music and language. Understand how rhythms influence sentence structures, phrasing, and speech patterns in Mandarin.

2. Melodic Intonation: Investigate thoroughly and deeply into the melodic intonation of Mandarin. Discover how pitch variations and musicality play a pivotal role in conveying emotions and intentions in speech.

Cultural Insights Through "Music and Language"

1. Musical Traditions: Recognize the influence of music on Mandarin culture. Learn how traditional melodies, folk songs, and contemporary tunes reflect historical narratives and cultural values.

2. Linguistic Melodies: Embrace the linguistic melodies of Mandarin. Analyze how the tonal system in Mandarin aligns with musical concepts, enhancing your tonal accuracy and comprehension.

Harmonious Learning in Action: Language-Music Fusion

1. Music Lyrics Translation: Engage in exercises that involve translating Mandarin song lyrics into your native language. This practice sharpens your translation skills while exposing you to cultural nuances.

2. Melodic Dialogues: Participate in melodic dialogue exercises. Practice speaking Mandarin sentences with melodic intonation to emulate the natural rhythms of spoken language.

Language Enhancement Through "Music and Language"

1. Lyric Analysis: Analyze the lyrics of Mandarin songs. Explore vocabulary, idiomatic expressions, and cultural references embedded in song lyrics to expand your linguistic knowledge.

2. Rhythmic Fluency: Experiment with rhythmic fluency exercises. Speak sentences with varying rhythms to develop your ability to adjust your speech pattern in different contexts.

Harmonious Learning in Action: Personal Musical Journey

1. Musical Exploration: Explore different genres of Mandarin music. Listen to classical, pop, rock, and folk music to experience the diverse linguistic and cultural expressions within each genre.

2. Musical Adaptation: Create musical adaptations of Mandarin sentences. Turn sentences into melodies to enhance your memorization of vocabulary and grammatical structures.

Practical Application and Melodic Mastery

1. Musical Conversation: Engage in conversations centered around musical and linguistic topics. Discuss the interplay between music and language, share favorite Mandarin songs, and exchange cultural insights.

2. Musical Language Exchange: Collaborate with language partners in musical language exchange sessions. Share songs, discuss lyrics, and practice speaking while embracing the musical and linguistic fusion.

Learning Beyond "Music and Language": Cultural Fusion

1. Music Appreciation: Attend Mandarin music concerts or events to immerse yourself in the cultural and linguistic aspects of Mandarin music. Observe how music serves as a bridge between language and artistic expression.

2. Cultural Discussions: Engage in conversations about the role of music in language learning. Explore how music enhances linguistic immersion, amplifies cultural understanding, and promotes cross-cultural connections.

Continued Harmonious Learning

As you work your way through the harmonious world of "Music and Language," let it resonate that your escapade is a continuous pursuit of understanding of auditory finesse, cultural resonance, and artistic integration. Harmonious Learning represents the continuous quest to infuse music into language learning, embrace the melodic essence of Mandarin, and experience the transformative power of harmonizing auditory and linguistic experiences.

By associating with in harmonious learning, you become a conductor of linguistic melodies, a harmonizer of auditory and linguistic realms, and a bridge between sound and expression. Each note you immerse yourself in becomes a testament to your linguistic journey, a resonance that harmonizes cross-cultural connections, and a tune that enriches your linguistic interactions and cultural appreciation.

Amid your unwavering commitment to linguistic and musical jaunt, may each melody you embrace be a reminder of the beauty of auditory language, a celebration of your commitment to harmonious learning, and a testament to the enduring impact of music in shaping our auditory perceptions and cross-cultural connections.

Cultivating Harmonious Learning

To further enrich your "Harmonious Learning" experience and cultivate the integration of Mandarin music into your language journey, consider these practical strategies:

1. Music Playlist: Create a Mandarin music playlist with a variety of genres. Listen to songs while commuting, exercising, or during leisure time to immerse yourself in the language's melodic rhythms.

2. Lyric Analysis: Analyze the lyrics of Mandarin songs. Break down idiomatic expressions, metaphors, and cultural references to expand your vocabulary and cultural insights.

3. Karaoke Practice: Sing along to Mandarin songs using karaoke apps or videos. Practice pronunciation, intonation, and rhythm while enjoying the musical experience.

4. Song Translation: Translate Mandarin song lyrics into your native language. This exercise enhances your translation skills and deepens your understanding of linguistic nuances.

Transferring Harmonious Learning Beyond Music

1. Musical Compositions: Create your own musical compositions using Mandarin lyrics. Experiment with melodies and rhythms to reinforce vocabulary and grammatical structures.

2. Music and Memory: Use Mandarin songs to aid memory retention. Associate vocabulary and phrases with specific melodies to *enhance* recall during language practice.

Unremitting Roam of Harmonious Mastery

During your passage through the harmonious world of "Music and Language," consider the fact that your wanderings are an ever-unfolding exploration of auditory immersion, cultural enrichment, and linguistic fusion. Harmonious Learning represents the continuous pursuit of harmonizing language and music, embracing melodic expressions, and experiencing the transformative power of auditory and linguistic integration.

By engrossing oneself in harmonious learning, you become a composer of linguistic melodies, a conductor of cultural resonance, and a bridge between auditory and linguistic dimensions. Each song you listen to becomes a testament to your linguistic journey, a musical thread that weaves through cross-cultural connections, and a harmonious note that enriches your linguistic interactions and cultural understanding.

While you continue your unwavering dedication to linguistic and musical cruise, may each melody you embrace be a reminder of the beauty of auditory language, a celebration of your dedication to harmonious learning, and a testament to the enduring impact of music in shaping our auditory perceptions and cross-cultural connections.

CHAPTER 27

Visual Vocabulary: Visualizing Words - Enhancing Vocabulary with Images

Commence an adventure in a vivid exploration of language and imagery with "Visual Vocabulary." Within this section, we immerse ourselves in the powerful connection between words and images, discovering how visual aids can elevate your Mandarin vocabulary learning. "Visualizing Words" is not just a lesson; it's a gallery of cognitive enhancement, cultural connection, and creative expansion. Through this learning-oriented exploration, you'll unravel the symbiotic relationship between language and visuals, develop strategies to integrate imagery into your vocabulary acquisition, and cultivate a profound connection with the Mandarin language. Get set to paint your learning journey with the colors of creativity and let your imagination enrich your linguistic progress.

The Essence of "Visual Vocabulary": Where Words Come to Life

1. Cognitive Engagement: "Visual Vocabulary" emphasizes the power of visual aids in engaging cognitive processes. By merging language with images, you create meaningful associations that enhance memory retention and understanding.

2. Cultural Context: Just as images reflect cultural nuances, they also enhance linguistic context. Delving into "Visualizing Words" offers insights into Mandarin linguistics, cultural symbolism, and the fusion of artistic expression.

Unraveling Visualizing Words: The Imagery-Language Nexus

1. Iconic Associations: Explore the concept of iconic associations. Learn how pairing images with vocabulary

words creates a mental bridge that facilitates quicker recall and comprehension.

2. Contextual Imagery: Uncover in detail the use of contextual imagery. Understand how visual aids can provide additional context to words, helping you grasp their meanings within sentences.

Cultural Insights Through "Visual Vocabulary"

1. Symbolic Imagery: Recognize the use of symbolism in Mandarin imagery. Explore how cultural symbols, historical references, and everyday objects enrich the meaning of vocabulary words.

2. Visual Cultural Expressions: Embrace the visual representations of Mandarin culture. Analyze how images reflect the essence of cultural identity, values, and societal customs.

Visualizing Words in Action: Language-Image Fusion

1. Image Flashcards: Create flashcards with vocabulary words on one side and corresponding images on the other. Review these flashcards regularly to reinforce associations between words and visuals.

2. Sentence Visualization: Engage in sentence construction using imagery. Craft sentences that incorporate vocabulary words and their visual counterparts to reinforce comprehension.

Language Enhancement Through "Visual Vocabulary"

1. Imaginative Writing: Practice imaginative writing using vocabulary words. Create short stories, descriptions, or scenarios that involve the use of vocabulary words and associated images.

2. Visual Mnemonics: Develop mnemonic techniques using images. Associate vocabulary words with memorable visuals to aid in word retention and recall.

Visualizing Words in Action: Personal Creative Exploration

1. Visual Vocabulary Art: Create visual artwork that embodies Mandarin vocabulary. Illustrate words and their meanings to connect visual and linguistic creativity.

2. Visual Word Mapping: Design visual word maps that showcase the interplay between vocabulary words and

related images. Use these maps as reference tools for learning and review.

Practical Application and Imaginative Mastery

1. Imaginative Conversation: Engage in conversations centered around vocabulary and imagery. Discuss the power of visual aids in language learning, share creative vocabulary associations, and explore the cultural significance of imagery.

2. Imaginative Language Exchange: Collaborate with language partners in imaginative language exchange sessions. Share vocabulary words, describe associated images, and engage in imaginative dialogues that enrich your linguistic and visual understanding.

Learning Beyond "Visual Vocabulary": Creative Exploration

1. Cultural Imagery: Explore imagery in Mandarin art, literature, and media. Examine how images are used to convey cultural narratives, historical events, and emotional depth.

2. Cultural Discussions: Engage in conversations about the role of imagery in language and culture. Explore how images enhance language learning, foster cultural connections, and deepen your appreciation for linguistic expression.

Continued Imaginative Mastery

As you chart your course through the vivid world of "Visual Vocabulary," always keep at heart that your pilgrimage is an ongoing unfolding of creative connection, cognitive enrichment, and linguistic fusion. Visualizing Words represents the continuous quest to merge language and imagery, embrace the art of visual association, and experience the transformative power of combining words with captivating visuals.

By engaging in visual vocabulary, you become an artist of linguistic expression, a curator of cognitive connections, and a bridge between words and images. Each visual association you create becomes a testament to your linguistic journey, a stroke of creativity that harmonizes cross-cultural connections, and an image that enriches your linguistic interactions and cultural appreciation.

In your continued commitment to creative and linguistic progression, may each visual association you form be a reminder of the beauty of imaginative language, a celebration of your commitment to visual vocabulary, and a testament to the enduring impact of images in shaping our cognitive perceptions and cross-cultural connections.

Cultivating Imaginative Mastery

To further delve into the enrichment of your "Visual Vocabulary" experience and cultivate imaginative mastery, consider these practical strategies:

1. Imagery Journal: Keep an imagery journal where you pair vocabulary words with visual representations. Write descriptions or stories for each image to reinforce your understanding.

2. Creative Flashcards: Design creative flashcards that go beyond literal images. Use metaphorical or abstract visuals to challenge your creative thinking while solidifying word associations.

3. Imaginary Scenarios: Invent imaginary scenarios that involve vocabulary words and their associated images. This

practice encourages you to think creatively and expand your vocabulary usage.

4. Word-Image Matching Games: Create interactive word-image matching games. Invite friends or language partners to match vocabulary words with corresponding visuals in an engaging and collaborative way.

Transferring Imaginative Mastery Beyond Language

1. Visual Storytelling: Develop short stories or comics that incorporate vocabulary words and their associated images. Practice narrative expression while reinforcing word comprehension.

2. Artistic Expression: Experiment with different art forms, such as drawing, painting, or digital design, to visually represent vocabulary words. Combine linguistic and artistic skills for a holistic learning experience.

Infinite Adventure of Imaginative Proficiency

As you navigate the imaginative world of "Visual Vocabulary," embrace the truth that your adventure is a lifelong journey of creative connection, cognitive enhancement, and linguistic innovation. Visualizing Words represents the continuous pursuit of merging language and imagery, embracing the power of visual association, and experiencing the transformative synergy of linguistic and visual artistry.

By participating in visual vocabulary, you become a conductor of imaginative symphonies, an architect of cognitive bridges, and a bridge between linguistic expression and visual representation. Each word-image association you craft becomes a testament to your linguistic journey, a brushstroke that weaves through the canvas of language, and an expression that enriches your linguistic interactions and cultural understanding.

During your unswerving creative and linguistic exploration, may each visual association you create be a reminder of the beauty of imaginative language, a celebration of your dedication to visual vocabulary, and a testament to the enduring impact of images in shaping our cognitive perceptions and cross-cultural connections.

CHAPTER 28

Culinary Connections: Taste of Mandarin - Learning Language Through Food

Initiate an endeavor in a delectable linguistic journey through cuisine with "Culinary Connections." In this chapter, we savor the rich flavors of Mandarin language learning by exploring the fascinating world of food. "Taste of Mandarin" is not just a lesson; it's a feast for the senses, a cultural exploration, and a culinary adventure. Through this learning-oriented exploration, you'll discover how food becomes a gateway to language, immerse yourself in the flavors of Mandarin culture, and cultivate a profound connection with the Mandarin language. Equip yourself to savor the blend of language and gastronomy as you step into the world of a unique path to linguistic mastery.

The Essence of "Culinary Connections": Where Language Meets Gastronomy

1. Sensory Engagement: "Culinary Connections" highlights the sensory engagement of language through food. By intertwining language and cuisine, you engage multiple senses, enhancing memory retention and cultural understanding.

2. Cultural Palate: Just as culinary traditions reflect cultural identity; they also offer insights into Mandarin culture. Delving into "Taste of Mandarin" provides a flavorful glimpse into Mandarin linguistics, culinary customs, and cross-cultural connections.

Unraveling Taste of Mandarin: The Gastronomic Language Fusion

1. Vocabulary Enrichment: Explore food-related vocabulary. Learn names of ingredients, dishes, cooking methods, and dining etiquettes to expand your Mandarin lexicon.

2. Culinary Context: Inspect meticulously into the context of culinary language. Understand how food-related phrases and idioms are used in daily conversations and literary expressions.

Cultural Insights Through "Culinary Connections"

1. Culinary Traditions: Recognize the significance of food in Mandarin culture. Explore how meals, festivals, and celebrations are intertwined with linguistic expressions and cultural practices.

2. Culinary Etiquette: Embrace the importance of culinary etiquette. Analyze how food-related customs, table manners, and social interactions reflect Mandarin cultural values.

Taste of Mandarin in Action: Language-Gastronomy Harmony

1. Food Vocabulary Practice: Engage in vocabulary-building exercises. Create flashcards, label kitchen items, and describe recipes to reinforce your knowledge of food-related words.

2. Culinary Conversations: Participate in food-themed dialogues. Practice ordering at restaurants, discussing recipes, and sharing dining experiences to enhance your conversational skills.

Language Enhancement Through "Culinary Connections"

1. Culinary Descriptions: Practice descriptive writing using food as a theme. Write detailed descriptions of dishes, flavors, and culinary experiences to refine your language skills.

2. Culinary Expressions: Explore idiomatic expressions related to food. Learn how idioms and phrases drawn from culinary experiences enrich your linguistic toolbox.

Taste of Mandarin in Action: Personal Gastronomic Exploration

1. Cooking Adventures: Experiment with cooking Mandarin recipes. Follow cooking videos or written recipes to not only learn about cuisine but also engage with culinary language.

2. Culinary Storytelling: Craft stories or narratives centered around food. Describe meals, share anecdotes, or invent culinary tales to practice language usage within a gastronomic context.

Practical Application and Gastronomic Proficiency

1. Culinary Conversations: Engage in conversations about food and culture. Discuss culinary traditions, share favorite

dishes, and exchange opinions on Mandarin cuisine to deepen your cultural and linguistic connections.

2. Culinary Language Exchange: Collaborate with language partners in culinary language exchange sessions. Share recipes, describe cooking techniques, and engage in gastronomic dialogues that enrich your language skills and cultural appreciation.

Learning Beyond "Culinary Connections": Cultural Immersion

1. Culinary Exploration: Attend Mandarin cooking classes, food festivals, or local markets to immerse yourself in the culinary and linguistic expressions of Mandarin cuisine.

2. Cultural Discussions: Engage in conversations about the role of food in language and culture. Explore how culinary language learning enhances cross-cultural connections, fosters appreciation for Mandarin heritage, and deepens your culinary understanding.

Continued Gastronomic Proficiency

Marching the course to the flavorful world of "Culinary Connections," stay conscious of the fact that your pursuit is an everlasting quest of sensory delight, cultural immersion, and linguistic savoring. Taste of Mandarin represents the continuous pursuit of intertwining language and gastronomy, embracing the flavorful essence of Mandarin culture, and experiencing the transformative synergy of culinary and linguistic exploration.

By taking part in culinary connections, you become a connoisseur of linguistic flavors, a culinary linguist, and a bridge between the world of language and the delights of cuisine. Each culinary term you master becomes a testament to your linguistic journey, a flavorful expression that bridges cross-cultural connections, and a taste that enriches your linguistic interactions and cultural understanding.

During your unflagging gastronomic and linguistic adventure, may each culinary experience you savor be a reminder of the beauty of sensory language, a celebration of your dedication to culinary connections, and a testament to the enduring impact of gastronomy in shaping our sensory perceptions and cross-cultural connections.

Cultivating Gastronomic Proficiency

To further enrich your "Culinary Connections" experience and cultivate gastronomic proficiency, consider these practical strategies:

1. Recipe Journal: Maintain a recipe journal where you write down Mandarin recipes along with their English translations. This practice not only enhances your vocabulary but also provides a collection of delicious dishes to try.

2. Culinary Cultural Exchange: Collaborate with Mandarin-speaking friends or language partners for a culinary cultural exchange. Share recipes from your culture and learn traditional Mandarin dishes, fostering linguistic and gastronomic connections.

3. Virtual Food Tours: Take virtual tours of Mandarin-speaking regions' culinary scenes. Explore local markets, street food stalls, and traditional restaurants through online videos, enhancing your cultural and language knowledge.

4. Culinary Storytelling: Incorporate food-related anecdotes and experiences into your Mandarin conversations and writing. Sharing personal culinary stories adds authenticity to your language usage.

Transferring Gastronomic Proficiency Beyond Language

1. Culinary Creativity: Experiment with creating fusion dishes that blend your cultural cuisine with Mandarin flavors. Describe your culinary experiments using Mandarin to expand your vocabulary.

2. Foodie Cultural Events: Attend food festivals or cultural events focused on Mandarin cuisine. Engage in conversations with chefs and attendees to further immerse yourself in the language and culture.

Infinite Travel of Gastronomic Delight

Progressing your way forward the flavorful world of "Culinary Connections," keep in mind that your travels represent an unending unfolding of sensory indulgence, cultural immersion, and linguistic fusion. Taste of Mandarin represents the continuous quest to merge language and gastronomy, embrace the richness of Mandarin cuisine, and experience the transformative synergy of culinary and linguistic exploration.

By joining in culinary connections, you become a culinary linguist, a cultural gastronome, and a bridge between the world of language and the delectable realm of cuisine. Each culinary term you master becomes a testament to your linguistic journey, a flavorful expression that bridges cross-cultural connections, and a taste that enriches your linguistic interactions and cultural appreciation.

While you proceed on your gastronomic and linguistic meander, may each bite you savor be a reminder of the beauty of sensory language, a celebration of your dedication to culinary connections, and a testament to the enduring impact of gastronomy in shaping our sensory perceptions and cross-cultural connections.

CHAPTER 29

Accent Mastery: Accent Symphony - Mastering Mandarin's Melodies

Commence an exploration of a melodic journey through the nuances of pronunciation with "Accent Mastery." In this chapter, we inspect closely into the captivating world of Mandarin accents, unraveling the intricate symphony of tones and intonations that shape the language. "Accent Symphony" is not just a lesson; it's a harmonious exploration, a cultural immersion, and a vocal adventure. Through this learning-oriented exploration, you'll discover the significance of accents, develop strategies for mastering Mandarin's tonal intricacies, and cultivate a profound connection with the melodious Mandarin language. Get ready to fine-tune your pronunciation and let the melodies guide your linguistic progress.

The Essence of "Accent Mastery": Where Sound Meets Expression

1. Aural Sensitivity: "Accent Mastery" underscores the importance of aural sensitivity in language learning. By delving into Mandarin's accent nuances, you train your ears to distinguish between tones and refine your pronunciation.

2. Cultural Harmony: Just as musical symphonies reflect cultural expressions; accents mirror the essence of Mandarin culture. Engaging in "Accent Symphony" offers insights into Mandarin linguistics, cultural contexts, and the fusion of vocal artistry.

Unraveling Accent Symphony: The Melodic Language Palette

1. Tonal Variation: Explore the tonal variation in Mandarin. Learn the four tones and their distinctive pitch patterns, understanding how they transform words and convey meanings.

2. Intonation Dynamics: Delve into intonation dynamics. Understand how the rise and fall of pitch patterns within sentences contribute to conveying questions, statements, and emotions.

Cultural Insights Through "Accent Mastery"

1. Linguistic Melodies: Recognize the significance of tonal harmony in Mandarin culture. Explore how tones influence communication, storytelling, and cultural expressions.

2. Intonation Nuances: Embrace the cultural nuances of intonation. Analyze how shifts in pitch convey politeness, emphasis, and social dynamics in Mandarin conversations.

Accent Symphony in Action: Tonal Precision

1. Tone Drills: Engage in daily tone drills. Practice pronouncing words with different tones to enhance your ability to differentiate and reproduce pitch patterns accurately.

2. Tonal Dialogues: Participate in tonal dialogues. Engage in conversations where tone variations play a pivotal role in conveying meaning and intention.

Language Enhancement Through "Accent Mastery"

1. Phonetic Accuracy: Focus on phonetic accuracy. Study the International Phonetic Alphabet (IPA) symbols for Mandarin to understand the exact sounds associated with each tone.

2. Accentuated Script: Practice reading Mandarin texts with tonal annotations. Highlight tone marks to reinforce your connection between written characters and their tonal pronunciations.

Accent Symphony in Action: Personal Melodic Exploration

1. Tonal Mimicry: Listen to native speakers and mimic their tonal patterns. Utilize language learning platforms that offer interactive pronunciation practice for accurate tonal reproduction.

2. Tonal Reflections: Record your voice while speaking Mandarin sentences. Listen to your pronunciation and compare it with native speakers to identify areas for improvement.

Practical Application and Vocal Harmony

1. Accentuated Conversation: Engage in conversations centered around tonal variation. Discuss the art of tonal

harmony, share experiences, and explore how accents contribute to linguistic richness.

2. Tonal Language Exchange: Collaborate with language partners in tonal language exchange sessions. Exchange sentences, practice tonal patterns, and engage in dialogues that enhance your tonal accuracy and cultural understanding.

Learning Beyond "Accent Mastery": Cultural Resonance

1. Tonal Melodies: Attend music performances or cultural events where tonal patterns are highlighted. Observe how tonal variations enrich musical compositions and cultural expressions.

2. Cultural Discussions: Engage in conversations about the role of accents in language and culture. Explore how tonal mastery enhances cross-cultural connections, fosters appreciation for Mandarin heritage, and deepens your linguistic understanding.

Continued Vocal Harmony

While traveling through the melodic world of "Accent Mastery," hold onto the concept that your expedition is a constant voyage of learning of auditory finesse, cultural immersion, and vocal artistry. Accent Symphony represents the continuous pursuit of mastering tonal nuances, harmonizing cross-cultural connections, and experiencing the transformative power of vocal expression.

By immersing oneself in accent mastery, you become a conductor of linguistic melodies, a vocal artist, and a bridge between the world of sound and the beauty of linguistic communication. Each tone you master becomes a testament to your linguistic journey, a melodic thread that weaves through cross-cultural connections, and a note that enriches your vocal interactions and cultural appreciation.

Amidst your ongoing devotion to vocal and linguistic traversal, may each tone you master be a reminder of the beauty of auditory language, a celebration of your dedication to accent mastery, and a testament to the enduring impact of vocal expression in shaping our auditory perceptions and cross-cultural connections.

Cultivating Vocal Harmony

To add depth to your "Accent Mastery" experience and cultivate vocal harmony, consider these practical strategies:

1. Tonal Shadowing: Engage in tonal shadowing exercises. Listen to native speakers and imitate their tonal patterns and intonations to refine your pronunciation.

2. Tonal Analysis: Analyze tonal patterns in Mandarin songs, movies, or speeches. Identify how tones contribute to emotional expression and convey cultural nuances.

3. Tone Clusters: Group words with similar tones together and practice saying them in rapid succession. This exercise enhances your ability to transition smoothly between tones.

4. Tonal Listening Practice: Listen to audio clips or podcasts featuring various speakers. Focus on distinguishing different tones in natural conversations.

Transferring Vocal Harmony Beyond Language

1. Melodic Speech: Experiment with incorporating tonal melodies into your speech. Express emotions, emphasize points, and engage in conversations with a heightened awareness of tonal variations.

2. Tonal Singing: Practice singing Mandarin songs to enhance your tonal accuracy. Singing allows you to focus on pitch variations and inflections in a musical context.

Unbroken Pilgrimage of Vocal Proficiency

Throughout your navigation of the melodic world of "Accent Mastery," it's important to maintain awareness that your voyage is a perpetual exploration of auditory precision, cultural immersion, and vocal mastery. Accent Symphony represents the continuous quest to harmonize tonal nuances, embrace the melodic intricacies of Mandarin, and experience the transformative synergy of vocal artistry and linguistic expression.

By indulging in accent mastery, you become a maestro of linguistic melodies, a conductor of vocal resonance, and a bridge between the world of sound and the captivating realm of language. Each tonal nuance you master becomes a testament to your linguistic journey, a melodic stroke that weaves through cross-cultural connections, and a pitch that enriches your vocal interactions and cultural understanding.

In your unwavering devotion to vocal and linguistic walkabout, may each tonal variation you perfect be a reminder of the beauty of auditory language, a celebration of your commitment to accent mastery, and a testament to the enduring impact of vocal expression in shaping our auditory perceptions and cross-cultural connections.

CHAPTER 30

Language Reflections: Journey's End - Reflecting on Progress and Growth

As your linguistic voyage draws to a close, set off for a reflective journey through "Language Reflections." In this final chapter, we traverse the terrain of self-assessment and introspection, looking back at the distance traveled, the milestones achieved, and the personal growth attained. "Journey's End" is not just a conclusion; it's a celebration of your linguistic quest, an opportunity to appreciate the progress made, and a stepping stone to continued language mastery. Through this learning-oriented exploration, you'll learn the art of self-evaluation, celebrate your achievements, and cultivate a profound connection with your linguistic journey. Be prepared to embrace the wisdom gained and set the stage for future language endeavors.

The Essence of "Language Reflections": Where Learning Meets Wisdom

1. Self-Awareness: "Language Reflections" underscores the importance of self-awareness in language learning. By looking back on your journey, you gain insights into your strengths, challenges, and learning preferences.

2. Personal Growth: Just as a journey shapes the traveler, your linguistic voyage shapes your personal growth. Engaging in "Journey's End" offers an opportunity to acknowledge the transformation you've undergone and the skills you've developed.

Unraveling Journey's End: The Path to Self-Evaluation

1. Progress Evaluation: Reflect on your language learning journey. Assess your proficiency in speaking, listening, reading, and writing Mandarin, identifying areas of improvement and mastery.

2. Cultural Connection: Examine your cultural immersion. Reflect on your understanding of Mandarin culture, customs,

and traditions, and acknowledge the cross-cultural connections you've established.

Cultural Insights Through "Language Reflections"

1. Linguistic Impact: Recognize the impact of language on cultural understanding. Explore how your language skills have deepened your appreciation for Mandarin heritage and bridged cross-cultural connections.

2. Personal Transformation: Embrace the personal transformation that comes with language learning. Analyze how linguistic growth has influenced your mindset, communication skills, and global perspective.

Journey's End in Action: Self-Appreciation and Goal Setting

1. Achievement Acknowledgment: Celebrate your linguistic achievements. Compile a list of milestones, such as holding conversations, reading Mandarin texts, or engaging with native speakers, to recognize your progress.

2. Goal Refinement: Set new language learning goals. Reflect on your current proficiency and identify areas you wish to focus on, whether it's perfecting certain aspects of

pronunciation, expanding your vocabulary, or delving deeper into cultural nuances.

Language Enhancement Through "Language Reflections"

1. Learning Strategies: Reflect on your learning strategies. Evaluate the effectiveness of your study methods, resources used, and language learning routines. Adjust your strategies based on what has worked well and areas that need improvement.

2. Self-Care and Language Learning: Recognize the importance of self-care in language learning. Reflect on how maintaining a healthy lifestyle, managing stress, and nurturing your well-being have influenced your learning experience.

Journey's End in Action: Personal Growth Celebration

1. Learning Journal: Review your language learning journal or notes. Observe how your thoughts, observations, and challenges have evolved throughout your journey, showcasing your linguistic and personal development.

2. Reflective Writing: Write a reflective essay or letter to yourself, summarizing your language learning experience. Express your emotions, share insights gained, and outline your aspirations for continued language growth.

Practical Application and Lifelong Learning

1. Language Legacy: Engage in conversations with fellow learners about your language journey. Share your experiences, challenges, and successes, contributing to a supportive language learning community.

2. Continued Exploration: Start an adventure into new language journeys. Apply the lessons learned from your Mandarin experience to other languages, embracing a lifelong commitment to multilingualism and cultural understanding.

Learning Beyond "Language Reflections": Lifelong Language Epic

1. Cultural Exploration: Continue your exploration of Mandarin culture. Engage in cultural events, read literature, and watch films to deepen your connection to Mandarin heritage and broaden your cultural perspective.

2. Cultural Conversations: Engage in conversations about language, culture, and personal growth. Share your reflections, discuss the transformative power of language learning, and inspire others to initiate a plunge into uncovering their own linguistic journeys.

Continued Self-Appreciation and Growth

As you move amidst the realm of "Language Reflections," reflect on the idea that your adventure is an eternal journey of growth of self-awareness, personal transformation, and lifelong learning. Journey's End represents not the conclusion of your language voyage, but the beginning of a new phase, enriched by your insights, achievements, and wisdom.

By embracing in language reflections, you become a scholar of self-discovery, a beacon of inspiration, and a bridge between personal growth and linguistic exploration. Each reflection you embrace becomes a testament to your journey, a guidepost that illuminates your path, and a legacy that enriches your linguistic interactions, personal development,

Throughout your undeterred reflective and linguistic campaign, may each insight gained be a reminder of the beauty of self-awareness, a celebration of your commitment to personal growth, and a testament to the enduring impact of language learning in shaping our identity, communication, and lifelong pursuit of knowledge.

Cultivating Lifelong Learning and Growth

For greater enhancement of your "Language Reflections" experience and cultivate lifelong learning and growth, consider these practical strategies:

1. Continued Learning: Embrace a mindset of continuous learning. Explore new aspects of Mandarin language and culture even after your initial journey. Stay curious and seek opportunities for deeper understanding.

2. Language Mentorship: Mentor fellow language learners. Share your experiences, provide guidance, and offer support to newcomers in their language learning journeys, fostering a sense of community and mutual growth.

3. Cultural Engagement: Attend cultural events and workshops related to Mandarin language and culture. Keep yourself immersed in the cultural context that nurtured your linguistic growth.

4. Multilingual Pursuits: Apply the skills and insights gained from Mandarin learning to other languages. Cultivate a diverse linguistic repertoire and gain a broader understanding of global communication.

Reflecting on the Odyssey of "Language Reflections"

As you reach the end of your linguistic voyage through "Language Reflections," take a moment to appreciate the transformation you've undergone, the knowledge you've acquired, and the connections you've forged. Your journey has been a symphony of dedication, curiosity, and growth, harmonizing linguistic exploration with personal development.

Language learning is not confined to vocabulary and grammar; it's a tapestry woven with cultural threads, self-discovery, and the intricate melodies of communication. Through "Language Reflections," you've embarked on a voyage that goes beyond words and phrases, transcending into a deeper understanding of yourself, your world, and the beauty of language as a bridge between cultures and minds.

As you stand at the crossroads of reflection and anticipation, remember that the journey you've undertaken is not an endpoint but a stepping stone to even greater horizons. Let the lessons, insights, and achievements of your Mandarin exploration guide you as you continue to explore, learn, and connect in the ever-expanding world of language and culture.

May your reflections be a testament to your dedication, your growth, and your unwavering commitment to the pursuit of knowledge, understanding, and connection. And as you set forth on new linguistic adventures, may each word spoken, each culture explored, and each connection made enrich your life and the lives of those you touch.

CHAPTER 31

Social Situations: Mingling and Making Friends - Conversations with Peers

Step into the vibrant realm of social interactions through "Social Situations." In this chapter, we immerse ourselves in the art of mingling and forging connections with peers, an essential aspect of language learning. "Mingling and Making Friends" isn't just a guide to socializing; it's a doorway to cultural understanding, a platform for authentic communication, and a catalyst for meaningful friendships. Through this learning-oriented exploration, you'll learn the dynamics of social conversations, navigate various contexts, and cultivate profound connections with peers. Prepare to set out on an expedition of camaraderie and cultural exchange.

The Essence of "Social Situations": Where Language Meets Relationships

1. Interpersonal Dynamics: "Social Situations" emphasizes the interpersonal dynamics of language learning. By engaging with peers, you practice language in authentic settings, fostering genuine connections.

2. Cultural Integration: Just as friendships bridge cultural divides, social interactions promote cultural integration. Embracing "Mingling and Making Friends" enhances your cultural awareness and sensitivity.

Unraveling Mingling and Making Friends: The Path to Social Fluency

1. Small Talk Mastery: Explore the art of small talk. Learn how to initiate conversations, maintain engagement, and transition between topics naturally.

2. Cultural Sensitivity: Delve into cultural sensitivity. Understand social customs, etiquette, and nuances that guide interactions in Mandarin-speaking contexts.

Cultural Insights Through "Social Situations"

1. Friendship Dynamics: Recognize the role of language in building friendships. Explore how language and shared experiences contribute to the formation of meaningful connections.

2. Cross-Cultural Bonding: Embrace cross-cultural bonding. Analyze how shared language experiences facilitate deeper understanding and rapport between individuals from diverse backgrounds.

Mingling and Making Friends in Action: Conversational Prowess

1. Group Conversations: Participate in group conversations. Engage in discussions, share opinions, and practice active listening within a social setting.

2. Casual Meetups: Attend casual meetups or language exchange events. Interact with peers, share experiences, and build connections through informal conversations.

Language Enhancement Through "Social Situations"

1. Expressive Communication: Enhance expressive communication skills. Practice articulating thoughts,

emotions, and opinions clearly and confidently in social contexts.

2. Slang and Informal Language: Familiarize yourself with slang and informal language. Learn expressions commonly used in casual conversations to further blend into social settings.

Mingling and Making Friends in Action: Friendship Forging

1. Personal Stories: Share personal stories and anecdotes. Discuss experiences, hobbies, and interests to establish common ground and strengthen connections.

2. Empathetic Listening: Practice empathetic listening. Pay attention to your peers' stories, opinions, and emotions, showing genuine interest and understanding.

Practical Application and Lasting Connections

1. Peer Language Exchange: Engage in peer language exchange partnerships. Collaborate with fellow learners to engage in meaningful language practice and cultural exchange.

2. Social Activities: Plan and participate in social activities. Join clubs, attend gatherings, or engage in shared hobbies to create authentic contexts for language use and friendship.

Learning Beyond "Social Situations": Lifelong Bonds

1. Cultural Exploration: Continue exploring Mandarin culture. Engage in cultural events, workshops, and activities with friends to deepen your connection and understanding.

2. Cultural Dialogues: Engage in conversations about friendships and language learning experiences. Share anecdotes, discuss cultural nuances, and inspire others to form cross-cultural connections.

Continued Social Fluency and Connection

Traveling through the exploration of the world of "Social Situations," allow the thought to linger that your pilgrimage is a continuous unfolding of interpersonal connections, cultural integration, and linguistic camaraderie. Mingling and Making Friends represents the continuous quest to blend language and relationships, embrace cultural diversity, and experience the transformative power of authentic interactions.

By engaging in social situations, you become a conversational connoisseur, a bridge builder, and a testament to the bonds forged through language and shared experiences. Each interaction you initiate becomes a testament to your linguistic journey, a thread that weaves through cross-cultural connections, and a memory that enriches your social interactions, personal growth, and cultural appreciation.

In your dedication to your social and linguistic trek, may each conversation you engage in be a reminder of the beauty of human connection, a celebration of your commitment to social fluency, and a testament to the enduring impact of authentic interactions in shaping our relationships, understanding, and lifelong friendships.

Cultivating Lasting Friendships and Cultural Exchange

To expand the richness of your "Social Situations" experience and cultivate lasting friendships and cultural exchange, consider these practical strategies:

1. Cultural Gatherings: Attend cultural events with friends. Explore festivals, exhibitions, or performances that

showcase Mandarin culture, providing opportunities for shared experiences and discussions.

2. Virtual Hangouts: Organize virtual hangouts with peers. Use online platforms to engage in video chats, games, or discussions, fostering connections even from different locations.

3. Cultural Potluck: Host a cultural potluck where friends bring dishes from their cultures. Share stories behind the food, discuss traditions, and engage in meaningful conversations.

4. Language and Film Nights: Arrange language and film nights with friends. Watch Mandarin movies or TV shows together, discussing plotlines, characters, and cultural aspects.

Transferring Social Fluency Beyond Language

1. Cultural Exchange Trips: Plan trips to Mandarin-speaking regions with friends. Immerse yourselves in local culture, engage with native speakers, and apply your language skills in real-life contexts.

2. Cultural Book Club: Start a cultural book club with friends. Choose Mandarin literature or translated works, read together, and hold discussions to deepen your understanding of cultural themes.

Unwavering Journey of Friendships and Connections

Progressing through and uncovering the landscape of "Social Situations," never let go of the idea that your tour is a constant exploration of human connections, cultural bridges, and the joy of shared experiences. Mingling and Making Friends represents not just a skill to master, but a lifelong pursuit of forming meaningful bonds and embracing the diversity of the world.

By being a part of social situations, you become a cultural ambassador, a friendship cultivator, and a bridge between languages and hearts. Each conversation you initiate becomes a testament to your linguistic journey, a gesture that transcends boundaries, and a reflection of the enduring impact of authentic interactions on our lives.

Amid your unwavering social and linguistic pilgrimage, may each connection you forge be a reminder of the beauty of friendship, a celebration of your commitment to cultural exchange, and a testament to the lasting impact of shared experiences in shaping our relationships, perspectives, and enriching the tapestry of our lives.

CHAPTER 32

Doctor Dialogues: Medical Mandarin - Navigating Health and Wellness

Enter the realm of health and wellness through "Doctor Dialogues." As this chapter unfolds, we dive into the crucial domain of medical Mandarin, equipping you with the language skills to effectively communicate with healthcare professionals and navigate health-related situations. "Medical Mandarin" isn't merely a lesson; it's a bridge to better healthcare access, a tool for clear communication, and a pathway to taking control of your well-being. Through this learning-oriented exploration, you'll master medical terminology, learn to articulate symptoms, and empower yourself to make informed health decisions. Ready yourself to begin a voyage of linguistic health literacy and improved healthcare interactions.

The Essence of "Doctor Dialogues": Where Language Meets Wellness

1. Health Literacy: "Doctor Dialogues" emphasizes the importance of health literacy in language learning. By mastering medical Mandarin, you enhance your ability to understand and discuss health-related topics.

2. Empowerment Through Communication: Just as understanding empowers patients, "Medical Mandarin" empowers you to communicate effectively with healthcare professionals, ensuring accurate diagnosis and treatment.

Unraveling Medical Mandarin: The Path to Health Communication

1. Medical Vocabulary: Explore essential medical vocabulary. Learn terms related to symptoms, diagnoses, treatments, and common health conditions.

2. Consultation Skills: Delve into effective consultation skills. Understand how to describe symptoms, provide medical history, and ask questions during healthcare interactions.

Cultural Insights Through "Doctor Dialogues"

1. Healthcare Practices: Recognize the cultural aspects of healthcare practices. Explore how language influences doctor-patient relationships, communication styles, and healthcare expectations.

2. Cross-Cultural Care: Embrace the role of language in cross-cultural healthcare. Analyze how linguistic proficiency fosters cultural understanding and respectful healthcare interactions.

Doctor Dialogues in Action: Health Conversation Mastery

1. Role-Play Exercises: Engage in role-play exercises. Practice doctor-patient scenarios, taking turns playing both roles to enhance your ability to communicate fluently.

2. Health Narratives: Narrate personal health experiences. Share stories of past health issues, treatments, and recoveries to practice articulating medical details.

Language Enhancement Through "Doctor Dialogues"

1. Medical Research: Deepen your understanding of medical terms. Research common health conditions and treatments, learning relevant vocabulary in context.

2. Medical Documents: Study medical documents in Mandarin. Read brochures, prescriptions, or health-related articles to familiarize yourself with medical language usage.

Doctor Dialogues in Action: Empowering Health Discussions

1. Doctor-Patient Interactions: Engage in real doctor-patient interactions. Attend medical appointments or health-related seminars where Mandarin is spoken, applying your language skills in practical settings.

2. Health Support Groups: Join health support groups conducted in Mandarin. Participate in discussions, share experiences, and seek advice within a supportive community.

Practical Application and Informed Wellness

1. Healthcare Resources: Explore healthcare resources in Mandarin. Familiarize yourself with medical websites, apps,

and resources available in the language for accurate health information.

2. Medical Consultation Preparation: Prepare for medical consultations. Write down symptoms, medical history, and questions in Mandarin before appointments to ensure effective communication.

Learning Beyond "Doctor Dialogues": Empowered Health Advocacy

1. Health Education: Continue your health education journey. Attend workshops, webinars, or courses in Mandarin to expand your knowledge of health and wellness.

2. Health Advocacy: Engage in health advocacy within Mandarin-speaking communities. Share your knowledge, promote health literacy, and empower others to navigate healthcare effectively.

Continued Health Communication Mastery

Navigating onward and discovering the realm of "Doctor Dialogues," reaffirm to yourself that your path is an unending exploration of possibilities of health literacy, cultural sensitivity, and informed wellness. Medical

Mandarin represents not just language proficiency, but a lifeline to better healthcare experiences, enhanced communication, and empowered health decisions.

Via your proactive involvement in doctor dialogues, you become a health communicator, a patient advocate, and a bridge between languages and healthcare access. Each health-related conversation you engage in becomes a testament to your linguistic journey, a tool that facilitates understanding, and a reflection of the profound impact of clear communication on our well-being.

In your unwavering health and linguistic voyage, may each health-related discussion you have be a reminder of the importance of health literacy, a celebration of your commitment to informed wellness, and a testament to the enduring impact of effective communication in shaping our health outcomes, relationships with healthcare professionals, and overall quality of life.

Cultivating Informed Health Advocacy and Communication

To deepen the enrichment of your "Doctor Dialogues" experience and cultivate informed health advocacy and communication, consider these practical strategies:

1. Health Journal: Keep a health journal in Mandarin. Document symptoms, treatments, and medical experiences to practice articulating health-related details.

2. Health Podcasts: Listen to health podcasts in Mandarin. Explore topics such as nutrition, exercise, and wellness, improving your listening skills while expanding your health knowledge.

3. Translate Medical Content: Translate medical content into Mandarin. Summarize health articles, medical guidelines, or research papers to enhance your language skills and health literacy.

4. Health Discussions: Initiate health discussions with native speakers. Engage in conversations about wellness, healthy habits, and medical topics to sharpen your communication abilities.

Transferring Health Communication Beyond Language

1. Health Seminars: Attend health seminars or workshops in Mandarin. Participate in discussions, ask questions, and learn from experts to broaden your health-related vocabulary.

2. Health Advocacy Groups: Join health advocacy groups conducted in Mandarin. Collaborate with others to raise awareness, share information, and promote health literacy within your community.

Unfaltering Trek of Health and Communication

Forging the journey to the world of "Doctor Dialogues," consider the journey as an ever-unfolding quest for personal growth of health empowerment, cultural understanding, and effective communication. Doctor Dialogues represents not just language proficiency, but a gateway to improved health outcomes, patient autonomy, and the empowerment of advocating for your well-being.

Via your genuine engagement in health communication, you become a health ambassador, a language advocate, and a testament to the transformative power of informed communication on our health and lives. Each health-related discussion you initiate becomes a testament to your linguistic journey, a conduit for sharing knowledge, and a reflection of the enduring impact of clear health communication on our individual and collective well-being.

As you continue your health and linguistic tour, may each health conversation you engage in be a reminder of the importance of health literacy, a celebration of your commitment to informed health advocacy, and a testament to the lasting impact of effective communication in shaping our health decisions, relationships with healthcare providers, and the pursuit of a healthier and more fulfilling life.

CHAPTER 33
Cultural Insights: Cultural Conundrums - Navigating Chinese Social Norms

Kickstart a pursuit of mastering the heart of Chinese social norms and cultural dynamics through "Cultural Insights." Herein, we delve into the intricacies of steering cultural nuances, fostering cross-cultural understanding, and adapting to Chinese social norms. "Cultural Conundrums" isn't just a cultural exploration; it's a key to building meaningful relationships, fostering respect, and deepening your connection to Mandarin-speaking communities. Through this learning-oriented exploration, you'll learn to navigate cultural intricacies, embrace diversity, and bridge the gap between languages and cultures. Gear up for the start of an adventure of cultural sensitivity and enriched cross-cultural interactions.

The Essence of "Cultural Insights": Where Language Meets Cultural Understanding

1. Cultural Sensitivity: "Cultural Insights" underscores the significance of cultural sensitivity in language learning. By delving into Chinese social norms, you enhance your ability to communicate respectfully and navigate cultural contexts.

2. Bridging Cultures Through Language: Just as words bridge languages, cultural understanding bridges cultures. Embracing "Cultural Conundrums" fosters connections, promotes harmony, and enriches your cross-cultural experiences.

Unraveling Cultural Conundrums: The Path to Cultural Integration

1. Cultural Norms: Explore essential Chinese cultural norms. Learn about greetings, social etiquette, gift-giving, and other customary practices to navigate interactions with respect.

2. Cultural Communication Styles: Delve into communication styles. Understand indirect communication,

nonverbal cues, and the importance of preserving face in Mandarin-speaking cultures.

Cultural Insights Through "Cultural Conundrums"

1. Social Harmony: Recognize the value of social harmony. Explore how cultural norms promote harmonious interactions, group cohesion, and mutual respect in Chinese societies.

2. Cultural Adaptation: Embrace the role of language in cultural adaptation. Analyze how linguistic proficiency facilitates smoother integration into Mandarin-speaking communities.

Cultural Conundrums in Action: Navigating Social Interactions

1. Cultural Role-Play: Engage in cultural role-play scenarios. Practice using appropriate greetings, expressions, and communication styles in various social contexts.

2. Cultural Etiquette Practice: Role-play cultural etiquette. Simulate scenarios involving dining, meetings, or gatherings to refine your understanding of cultural norms.

Language Enhancement Through "Cultural Conundrums"

1. Cultural Vocabulary: Deepen your cultural vocabulary. Study idiomatic expressions, proverbs, and slang that reveal cultural insights and enhance your language proficiency.

2. Cultural Context Reading: Read literature and articles about Chinese culture. Contextualize language use within cultural narratives, gaining a deeper understanding of social norms

Cultural Conundrums in Action: Cross-Cultural Engagement

1. Cultural Events: Attend cultural events and festivals. Engage in conversations with native speakers, immersing yourself in cultural discussions and understanding the significance behind customs.

2. Cross-Cultural Interviews: Conduct cross-cultural interviews. Speak with Mandarin-speaking individuals about their cultural experiences, fostering a deeper appreciation for diversity.

Practical Application and Intercultural Harmony

1. Cultural Reflection Journal: Keep a cultural reflection journal. Document your experiences, observations, and reflections on directing Chinese social norms to track your growth.

2. Cross-Cultural Sharing: Share your insights with others. Engage in discussions, blog posts, or presentations about Chinese cultural norms, promoting intercultural dialogue.

Learning Beyond "Cultural Insights": Global Citizenship

1. Comparative Cultural Exploration: Continue exploring cultural norms. Compare Chinese social norms with those of other cultures, broadening your understanding of global diversity.

2. Cultural Sensitivity Advocacy: Advocate for cultural sensitivity. Participate in discussions, workshops, or events that promote cross-cultural understanding and respect.

Continued Cultural Sensitivity and Connection

Piloting the way forward to the landscape of "Cultural Insights," remember that your journey is an ongoing exploration of cultural empathy, intercultural communication, and global citizenship. Cultural Conundrums represents not just an understanding of customs, but a gateway to deepening connections, promoting respect, and fostering a harmonious coexistence among diverse cultures.

By involving yourself in cultural insights, you become a cultural bridge builder, an advocate for understanding, and a testament to the transformative power of cultural sensitivity on our relationships, global perspective, and the enrichment of the human experience. Each cultural interaction you engage in becomes a testament to your linguistic journey, a bridge that connects cultures, and a reflection of the enduring impact of cross-cultural awareness on our interconnected world.

As you journey on in your cultural and linguistic tour, may each cross-cultural encounter you embrace be a reminder of the beauty of diversity, a celebration of your commitment to cultural empathy, and a testament to the lasting impact of intercultural communication in shaping our relationships, perspectives, and fostering a more inclusive global society.

Cultivating Cross-Cultural Harmony and Understanding

For additional refinement of your "Cultural Insights" experience and cultivate cross-cultural harmony and understanding, consider these practical strategies:

1. Cultural Exchange Partnerships: Engage in cross-cultural exchange partnerships. Connect with native Mandarin speakers and share insights about your own culture while learning about theirs.

2. Cultural Workshops: Attend cultural workshops and seminars. Participate in discussions, activities, and workshops that focus on promoting cross-cultural understanding and appreciation.

3. Cultural Challenges: Embrace cultural challenges intentionally. Seek out situations that require you to navigate Chinese social norms, such as attending gatherings or participating in traditional events.

4. Cultural Mentorship: Find a cultural mentor. Establish a relationship with someone who can guide you through the intricacies of Chinese social norms and provide insights into cultural dynamics.

Transferring Cultural Sensitivity Beyond Language

1. Cultural Writing: Write about your cultural experiences. Share stories, reflections, or observations about your interactions with Chinese social norms to deepen your cultural understanding.

2. Cultural Diversity Promotion: Organize cultural diversity events. Host gatherings, presentations, or cultural showcases to promote cross-cultural understanding within your community.

Constant Itinerary of Cross-Cultural Understanding

Trekking the path to the world of "Cultural Insights," remember that your journey is an ongoing exploration of cultural empathy, intercultural growth, and global citizenship. Cultural Conundrums represents not just an understanding of social norms, but a lifelong commitment to fostering cross-cultural harmony and mutual respect.

Via your participation in cultural insights, you become a cultural ambassador, a bridge between languages and cultures, and a testament to the enduring impact of cultural sensitivity on our interconnected world. Each cross-cultural interaction you initiate becomes a testament to your linguistic journey, a catalyst for meaningful connections, and a reflection of the profound influence of cultural understanding on our shared human experience.

In your committed journey towards cultural and linguistic exploration, may each cultural encounter you embrace be a reminder of the beauty of diverse perspectives, a celebration of your commitment to cross-cultural understanding, and a testament to the lasting impact of intercultural communication in shaping our relationships, fostering global harmony, and creating a world that embraces its rich tapestry of cultures.

CHAPTER 34

Expressions Unleashed: Speaking Like a Native - An Expressions Extravaganza

Venture forth into exploring a thrilling journey of linguistic finesse and cultural immersion through "Expressions Unleashed." Within the sphere of this chapter, we are to explore the captivating world of mastering expressions, allowing you to speak Mandarin with the nuance and flair of a native speaker. "Expressions Extravaganza" is not merely a lesson in language; it's a gateway to cultural authenticity, effective communication, and the art of nuanced expression. Through this learning-oriented adventure, you'll unearth a treasure trove of idioms, phrases, and colloquialisms that breathe life into your conversations. Prepare to unlock the power of vivid communication and deepen your connection to Mandarin-speaking communities.

The Essence of "Expressions Unleashed": Elevating Language Proficiency

1. Expressive Fluency: "Expressions Unleashed" underscores the importance of expressive fluency in language learning. By mastering idiomatic expressions, you elevate your ability to communicate nuances effectively.

2. Cultural Connection: Just as idioms are rooted in culture, your proficiency in them fosters a deeper cultural connection. Embracing "Expressions Extravaganza" enables you to engage meaningfully within Mandarin-speaking contexts.

Unveiling Expressions Extravaganza: The Path to Nuanced Communication

1. Idiomatic Riches: Delve into a treasury of idiomatic expressions. Explore their meanings, origins, and usage, allowing you to communicate like a true native.

2. Contextual Mastery: Develop an acute understanding of context. Learn to wield expressions appropriately in various conversational settings for impactful communication.

Cultural Insights Through "Expressions Unleashed"

1. Cultural Nuances: Recognize the cultural nuances within expressions. Explore how idioms embody shared values, historical references, and societal dynamics.

2. Cultural Sensitivity: Embrace the role of cultural sensitivity in idiomatic usage. Analyze how linguistic proficiency enhances your grasp of cultural subtleties.

Expressions Extravaganza in Action: Mastering Idiomatic Usage

1. Idiom Integration: Engage in immersive idiom integration exercises. Practice using idiomatic expressions in sentences, dialogues, and narratives to refine your fluency.

2. Everyday Idiom Integration: Apply idioms to daily conversations. Challenge yourself to use idiomatic expressions in casual interactions, gradually incorporating them into your speech.

Language Enhancement Through "Expressions Unleashed"

1. Etymology Exploration: Deepen your understanding of idioms' origins. Research the historical and cultural context that shaped idiomatic phrases to enrich your linguistic proficiency.

2. Idiomatic Reading: Read books, articles, or stories with idiomatic expressions. Uncover idioms in their natural context, observing how they enhance narrative depth.

Expressions Extravaganza in Action: Enriching Conversations

1. Expressive Storytelling: Tell stories with idiomatic flair. Craft narratives that incorporate idiomatic expressions, elevating your storytelling prowess and engaging your audience.

2. Idiomatic Discussions: Engage in idiomatic discussions. Initiate conversations centered around idioms, their meanings, and their relevance in contemporary society.

Practical Application and Linguistic Artistry

1. Idiom Journal: Keep an idiom journal. Document idioms you encounter, their meanings, and instances of their usage to track your progress.

2. Idiomatic Creativity: Create your own idiomatic expressions. Playfully invent idioms that encapsulate specific emotions or situations, showcasing your linguistic creativity.

Learning Beyond "Expressions Unleashed": Linguistic Flourish

1. Comparative Idiom Analysis: Expand your idiom repertoire. Compare idiomatic expressions across languages, delving into the cultural nuances they reflect.

2. Idiomatic Poetry: Write idiomatic poetry. Craft poems that feature idioms, harnessing their evocative power to convey intricate emotions and vivid imagery.

Continued Expressive Excellence and Fluency

Traversing onward the realm of "Expressions Unleashed," don't underestimate the lifelong nature of your pursuit's unfolding of linguistic artistry, cultural depth, and nuanced communication. "Expressions Extravaganza" represents not just mastery of phrases, but a continual quest to infuse your language with authenticity, richness, and an innate understanding of cultural nuances.

By immersing yourself in idiomatic expressions, you become a linguistic virtuoso, a cultural ambassador, and a testament to the profound impact of expressive communication on our relationships, perspectives, and the vibrant tapestry of human expression. Each idiomatic utterance you deliver becomes a testament to your linguistic journey, a brushstroke that adds depth to your conversations, and a reflection of the enduring influence of nuanced expression on our interconnected world.

Amid your unyielding expressive and linguistic trip, may each idiomatic encounter you embrace be a celebration of cultural intricacies, an embodiment of your dedication to linguistic finesse, and a testament to the lasting impact of expressive communication in shaping our interactions, fostering cultural connections, and elevating the beauty of human language.

Cultivating Idiomatic Mastery and Authenticity

To enhance and enrich your "Expressions Unleashed" experience and cultivate idiomatic mastery and authenticity, consider these practical strategies:

1. Idiomatic Conversations: Engage in idiomatic conversations with native speakers. Practice using idioms in real-life discussions, seeking feedback on proper usage and nuances.

2. Idiomatic Media Consumption: Consume idiomatic content. Watch movies, TV shows, or podcasts in Mandarin that feature idiomatic expressions, enhancing your listening skills while expanding your idiomatic repertoire.

3. Idiomatic Writing: Incorporate idioms into your writing. Craft essays, stories, or blog posts that employ idiomatic expressions, showcasing your ability to seamlessly integrate them into written communication.

4. Idiomatic Reflection: Reflect on idiomatic encounters. After conversations or interactions, jot down instances where you used or encountered idioms, along with your thoughts on their impact.

Transferring Idiomatic Proficiency Beyond Language

1. Idiomatic Workshops: Attend idiomatic workshops or seminars. Participate in sessions that delve deeper into the origins, meanings, and cultural significance of idiomatic expressions.

2. Idiomatic Creative Projects: Initiate idiomatic creative projects. Collaborate with fellow learners to create idiomatic comics, videos, or art pieces that celebrate the art of expressions.

Ageless Itinerary of Expressive Fluency

Steering through and uncovering the realm of "Expressions Unleashed," reflect on the reality that your pursuit is an everlasting journey of linguistic artistry, cultural insight, and personal growth. "Expressions Extravaganza" signifies not just mastery of phrases, but a commitment to harnessing language as a tool for authentic and nuanced communication.

Through your active involvement in idiomatic expressions, you become a master of linguistic subtleties, a cultural ambassador, and a testament to the transformative power of expressive communication on our relationships, connections, and understanding of diverse cultures. Each idiomatic phrase you incorporate becomes a testament to your linguistic journey, a brushstroke that paints a vivid picture of your conversations, and a reflection of the enduring influence of idiomatic fluency on our interconnected world.

During your relentless expressive and linguistic voyage, may each idiomatic encounter you embrace be a celebration of linguistic diversity, an embodiment of your dedication to idiomatic mastery, and a testament to the lasting impact of expressive communication in shaping our interactions, fostering cross-cultural connections, and adding vibrancy to the symphony of human expression.

CHAPTER 35

Travel Tales: Engaging Travel Conversations - Roaming China

Commence an exhilarating expedition of language and culture through "Travel Tales." In this chapter, we venture into the world of travel conversations, enabling you to navigate China with confidence and connect with locals on a deeper level. "Roaming China" is not just a travel guide; it's a key to immersive language acquisition, cultural exploration, and meaningful interactions. Through this learning-oriented voyage, you'll equip yourself with essential travel vocabulary, master practical dialogues, and unlock the gateway to unforgettable experiences. Prepare to start an unforgettable journey of linguistic enrichment and cultural immersion.

The Essence of "Travel Tales": Exploring China Through Language

1. Practical Proficiency: "Travel Tales" emphasizes practical language proficiency. By mastering travel-related vocabulary and dialogues, you empower yourself to navigate real-world situations effectively.

2. Cultural Engagement: Just as travel expands horizons, your language skills deepen cultural engagement. Embracing "Roaming China" empowers you to bridge cultural gaps and connect authentically with locals.

Embarking on "Roaming China": Your Guide to Travel Conversations

1. Travel Vocabulary: Dive into a treasure trove of travel-related vocabulary. Learn essential phrases for directions, transportation, accommodations, and everyday interactions.

2. Navigational Skills: Develop adept navigational skills. Familiarize yourself with asking for directions, reading signs, and understanding transportation options.

Cultural Insights Through "Roaming China"

1. Cultural Sensitivity in Travel: Recognize cultural nuances while traveling. Explore how cultural understanding shapes interactions, etiquette, and experiences during your journey.

2. Cultural Etiquette: Embrace cultural etiquette in travel conversations. Analyze how linguistic proficiency enhances your respect for local customs and fosters positive interactions.

"Roaming China" in Action: Mastering Travel Dialogues

1. Scenario-Based Practice: Engage in immersive travel scenario practice. Role-play dialogues for purchasing tickets, ordering food, checking in at hotels, and more.

2. Interactive Simulations: Simulate travel situations. Use dialogues to navigate scenarios like shopping, sightseeing, or seeking assistance, refining your conversational skills.

Language Enhancement Through "Travel Tales"

1. Cultural and Historical Reading: Enhance your knowledge of Chinese culture and history. Read about landmarks, traditions, and local customs to enrich your travel conversations.

2. Real-Life Materials: Use real travel materials. Study maps, brochures, menus, and signs in Mandarin to prepare for real-world travel encounters.

"Roaming China" in Action: Real Travel Experiences

1. Travel Diaries: Document your travel experiences. Write travel diaries in Mandarin, describing encounters, places visited, and cultural insights to reinforce your language skills.

2. Local Interactions: Engage in conversations with locals. Practice your travel dialogues with native speakers, enhancing your communication skills and cultural understanding.

Practical Application and Cultural Exploration

1. Travel Blogging: Start a travel blog. Share your journey, experiences, and language progress, connecting with a community of fellow travelers and language enthusiasts.

2. Travel Photography: Capture your experiences through photography. Use captions and descriptions in Mandarin to document your travels and express your impressions.

Learning Beyond "Travel Tales": Globetrotting Linguist

1. Cross-Cultural Comparisons: Expand your travel vocabulary. Compare travel-related phrases across languages, exploring linguistic diversity and cultural similarities.

2. Multilingual Travel: Learn travel phrases in multiple languages. Compare linguistic approaches to travel communication, fostering cross-cultural understanding.

Continued Travel Conversations and Linguistic Exploration

Advancing through and finding the world of "Travel Tales," it's worth remembering that your pilgrimage is a lifelong exploration of linguistic versatility, cultural immersion, and enriching experiences. "Roaming China" signifies not just travel preparation, but a continual quest to engage with the world, bridge language barriers, and connect with diverse communities.

Through your enthusiastic participation in travel conversations, you become a cultural explorer, a linguistic ambassador, and a testament to the transformative power of language on our travel experiences, cultural understanding, and the enrichment of human connections. Each travel dialogue you engage in becomes a testament to your linguistic journey, a compass guiding you through new territories, and a reflection of the enduring influence of language on our global exploration.

While you carry forward your mission to travel and linguistic quest, may each travel conversation you embark upon be a celebration of cross-cultural connections, an embodiment of your dedication to language learning, and a testament to the lasting impact of communication in shaping our travel experiences, fostering cultural engagement, and creating a world united by the beauty of diverse languages.

Cultivating Travel Fluency and Cultural Immersion

To further enhance your "Travel Tales" experience and cultivate travel fluency and cultural immersion, consider these practical strategies:

1. Travel Language Partners: Connect with travel language partners. Engage in language exchange with native Mandarin speakers who are eager to learn your language as well.

2. Local Cultural Experiences: Immerse yourself in local culture. Participate in traditional activities, festivals, or

workshops during your travels to deepen your understanding and language application.

3. Cultural Tours: Join guided cultural tours. Participate in tours led by local experts to gain insights into the historical, social, and cultural context of the places you visit.

4. Culinary Adventures: Explore local cuisine. Use your travel vocabulary to order food in Mandarin and engage with local restaurant staff, enhancing your language skills while savoring new flavors.

Transferring Travel Fluency Beyond Language

1. Travel Blogging in Mandarin: Start a travel blog in Mandarin. Share your experiences, photos, and language progress, connecting with a global audience interested in travel and language learning.

2. Cultural Exchange Projects: Initiate cultural exchange projects. Collaborate with language learners from different countries to create a multilingual travel resource.

Time-honored Pathway of Travel Conversations

As you journey through the world of "Travel Tales," remember that your adventure is a continuous exploration of linguistic versatility, cultural immersion, and global connection. "Roaming China" signifies not just travel preparation, but an ongoing commitment to expanding your horizons, embracing new cultures, and fostering meaningful connections.

Via your deep engagement in travel conversations, you become a global wanderer, a cultural ambassador, and a testament to the profound impact of language on our travel experiences, intercultural understanding, and the enrichment of human connections. Each travel dialogue you initiate becomes a testament to your linguistic journey, a ticket to immersive experiences, and a reflection of the enduring influence of language in shaping our exploration of the world.

In your ongoing quest for travel and linguistic discovery, may each travel conversation you embark upon be a celebration of cultural diversity, an embodiment of your dedication to linguistic enrichment, and a testament to the lasting impact of communication in shaping our travel encounters, fostering cross-cultural engagement, and creating a world united by the shared love of languages and exploration.

CHAPTER 36

Techno Talk: Navigating the Digital Landscape - Tech Lingo

Set out upon a course towards an exciting journey through the realm of technology and language with "Techno Talk." Amidst the material of this chapter, we are to examine the dynamic world of tech lingo, equipping you with the linguistic tools to navigate the digital landscape with ease. "Tech Lingo" is not just a lesson in vocabulary; it's a key to technological fluency, enhanced communication, and active participation in the digital age. Through this learning-oriented adventure, you'll unravel the complexities of tech terms, embrace digital culture, and empower yourself to engage confidently in tech-related discussions. Prepare to begin a voyage towards achieving a fascinating exploration of language and innovation.

The Essence of "Techno Talk": Bridging Language and Technology

1. Linguistic Tech Proficiency: "Techno Talk" highlights the importance of linguistic tech proficiency. By mastering tech terminology, you unlock the ability to communicate effectively in the digital sphere.

2. Digital Literacy: Just as language empowers, technological literacy propels you forward. Embracing "Tech Lingo" empowers you to bridge the digital divide and engage confidently in tech conversations.

Navigating the Digital Landscape: Unveiling "Tech Lingo"

1. Tech Vocabulary: Dive into a comprehensive array of tech-related vocabulary. Learn terms related to devices, software, programming, and online interactions.

2. Digital Communication: Develop your digital communication skills. Familiarize yourself with tech jargon commonly used in emails, messages, and online platforms.

Cultural Insights Through "Tech Lingo"

1. Tech in Cultural Context: Recognize the cultural context of tech terminology. Explore how digital culture shapes language and influences online interactions.

2. Tech Ethics and Etiquette: Embrace tech ethics and etiquette. Analyze how linguistic proficiency enhances your ability to navigate online spaces respectfully.

"Tech Lingo" in Action: Mastering Digital Conversations

1. Digital Scenario Practice: Engage in immersive digital scenario practice. Role-play tech-related dialogues, troubleshooting conversations, and online interactions.

2. Interactive Tech Simulations: Simulate tech interactions. Use dialogues to navigate scenarios like troubleshooting, customer support, or collaborative online projects.

Language Enhancement Through "Techno Talk"

1. Tech Reading: Enhance your understanding of tech concepts. Read tech articles, blogs, or documentation to familiarize yourself with advanced tech terms and discussions.

2. Tech Media Consumption: Immerse yourself in tech media. Watch tech videos, podcasts, or TED talks in Mandarin to absorb tech lingo within relevant contexts.

"Tech Lingo" in Action: Embracing Digital Culture

1. Tech Blogging: Start a tech-focused blog. Share insights, reviews, or tips related to technology in Mandarin, engaging with fellow tech enthusiasts.

2. Tech Discussion Groups: Join tech discussion groups or forums. Participate in online tech communities where you can discuss tech trends, innovations, and insights in Mandarin.

Practical Application and Digital Empowerment

1. Tech Documentation Translation: Translate tech documentation. Choose a tech manual or guide, and translate it into Mandarin, enhancing your tech vocabulary and language proficiency.

2. Tech Project Collaboration: Collaborate on tech projects. Work with fellow learners to develop tech-related content, websites, or apps entirely in Mandarin.

Learning Beyond "Techno Talk": Technological Fluency

1. Cross-Linguistic Tech Comparison: Expand your tech vocabulary. Compare tech terms across languages, exploring linguistic nuances and technological innovation.

2. Multilingual Coding: Learn coding terminology in Mandarin. Compare coding languages and terms, gaining a deeper understanding of tech language diversity.

Continued Technological Fluency and Linguistic Exploration

Journeying steadily through the world of "Techno Talk," don't lose sight of the fact that your venture is an ongoing pursuit of linguistic innovation, digital empowerment, and global connection. "Tech Lingo" signifies not just tech literacy, but an enduring commitment to embracing technological advancements, bridging language gaps, and participating actively in the digital world.

Through your thorough engagement in tech conversations, you become a digital trailblazer, a linguistic navigator, and a testament to the transformative power of language in our digital interactions, cultural understanding, and the advancement of human connectivity. Each tech dialogue you initiate becomes a testament to your linguistic journey, a keystroke that contributes to technological progress, and a reflection of the enduring influence of linguistic tech proficiency on our interconnected digital realm.

During your undaunted technological and linguistic march, may each tech conversation you engage in be a celebration of digital diversity, an embodiment of your dedication to tech language learning, and a testament to the lasting impact of communication in shaping our digital interactions, fostering tech literacy, and creating a world united by the shared language of technology.

Cultivating Technological Fluency and Digital Engagement

To further enhance your "Techno Talk" experience and cultivate technological fluency and digital engagement, consider these practical strategies:

1. Tech Podcasts: Listen to tech podcasts in Mandarin. Immerse yourself in discussions on tech trends, innovations, and debates to enhance your listening skills and tech vocabulary.

2. Tech Webinars: Attend tech webinars or online workshops. Participate in virtual tech events conducted in Mandarin to stay updated on the latest tech developments.

3. Online Coding Platforms: Explore online coding platforms in Mandarin. Learn coding while immersing yourself in tech-related vocabulary and instructions.

4. App Localization: Participate in app localization. Collaborate with developers to translate apps or software into Mandarin, deepening your understanding of tech language.

Transferring Technological Fluency Beyond Language

1. Tech Blog Collaboration: Collaborate with tech bloggers. Co-author tech-related articles or blog posts in Mandarin, exchanging insights and sharing your expertise.

2. Tech Innovations in Other Cultures: Explore tech innovations in other cultures. Research tech trends and innovations from Mandarin-speaking regions, comparing and contrasting with your own.

Continuous Sojourn of Techno Talk

As you progress through the world of "Techno Talk," remember that your journey is a continuous exploration of technological literacy, digital integration, and global communication. "Tech Lingo" signifies not just a linguistic adventure, but an ongoing commitment to adapting to technological advancements, embracing digital culture, and fostering connections through language.

Through your engagement in tech conversations, you become a digital ambassador, a linguistic innovator, and a testament to the profound influence of language on our technological interactions, cross-cultural understanding, and the advancement of our digital society. Each tech term you learn becomes a testament to your linguistic journey, a code that unlocks new possibilities, and a reflection of the enduring impact of technological fluency on our interconnected digital world.

While you advance on your path of technological and linguistic escapade, may each tech conversation you participate in be a celebration of digital inclusivity, an embodiment of your dedication to tech language mastery, and a testament to the lasting impact of communication in shaping our digital experiences, fostering tech literacy, and creating a world united by the shared language of technology.

CHAPTER 37
Language Play: Mastering Sounds - Tongue Twisters and Challenges

Prepare to take the first steps in grasping a whimsical and engaging journey through the world of linguistic exploration with "Language Play." Within these pages, we shall probe into the captivating realm of tongue twisters, phonetic challenges, and auditory acrobatics, equipping you with the tools to master sounds and enhance your language skills. "Tongue Twisters and Challenges" are not mere linguistic exercises; they are keys to refining pronunciation, improving enunciation, and embracing the joy of playful language. Through this learning-oriented escapade, you'll unlock the secrets of phonetics, nurture a keen ear for linguistic subtleties, and revel in the art of mastering sounds. Get set to initiate a quest an unforgettable voyage of linguistic delight.

The Essence of "Language Play": Unveiling Phonetic Proficiency

1. Sound Mastery: "Language Play" underscores the significance of sound mastery. By entering into playful phonetic challenges, you unlock the ability to articulate sounds with precision and flair.

2. Phonetic Fluency: Just as language flows, phonetic fluency enhances communication. Embracing "Tongue Twisters and Challenges" empowers you to captivate listeners with impeccable pronunciation.

Navigating "Tongue Twisters and Challenges": Embracing Phonetic Prowess

1. Tongue Twister Delight: Dive into a captivating collection of tongue twisters. Explore phrases designed to challenge your articulation, rhythm, and sound differentiation.

2. Enunciation Excellence: Develop impeccable enunciation skills. Practice articulating sounds, vowels, and consonants

clearly and distinctively, enhancing your oral communication.

Cultural Insights Through "Language Play

1. Cultural Tongue Twisters: Discover cultural tongue twisters. Explore how different languages and cultures use similar linguistic devices, providing insights into linguistic commonalities.

2. Phonetic Nuances in Languages: Recognize phonetic nuances in different languages. Analyze how specific sounds and phonetic patterns contribute to the distinctive quality of various languages.

"Tongue Twisters and Challenges" in Action: Mastering Phonetic Precision

1. Phonetic Drill Exercises: Engage in immersive phonetic drills. Practice repeating challenging sounds, combinations, and phrases to fine-tune your pronunciation.

2. Tongue Twister Performance: Perform tongue twisters confidently. Recite tongue twisters with varying tempos and dynamics, showcasing your phonetic prowess.

Language Enhancement Through "Language Play"

1. Phonetic Listening Practice: Hone your listening skills. Listen to native speakers recite tongue twisters or challenging phrases, refining your ability to distinguish subtle sound variations.

2. Phonetic Mimicry: Mimic native speakers. Use audio resources to imitate native pronunciation, infusing your speech with authentic phonetic qualities.

"Tongue Twisters and Challenges" in Action: Expressive Delivery

1. Tongue Twister Storytelling: Create narratives using tongue twisters. Craft imaginative stories that incorporate challenging phrases, showcasing your ability to weave playful language into storytelling.

2. Phonetic Diction in Speech: Incorporate tongue twister principles into daily speech. Practice delivering clear and melodious sentences, enhancing your overall linguistic fluency.

Practical Application and Artistic Expression

1. Tongue Twister Recordings: Record tongue twister performances. Create audio recordings of your tongue twister recitations, tracking your progress and sharing them with language partners.

2. Phonetic Artistry: Engage in phonetic art projects. Create visual representations of tongue twisters, combining linguistic and artistic elements for a unique form of expression.

Learning Beyond "Language Play": Phonetic Artistry

1. Phonetic Music Fusion: Combine phonetics and music. Experiment with creating melodies or rhythms using tongue twister phrases, exploring the interplay of sound and musicality.

2. Cross-Linguistic Phonetic Comparisons: Explore phonetic variations across languages. Compare tongue twisters in Mandarin with those in your native language, uncovering the intricacies of phonetic diversity.

Continued Phonetic Mastery and Linguistic Exploration

As you journey through the world of "Language Play," remember that your adventure is a continuous exploration of phonetic finesse, artistic expression, and language playfulness. "Tongue Twisters and Challenges" signify not just linguistic exercise, but a lifelong commitment to perfecting sounds, embracing linguistic creativity, and enhancing your overall communication skills.

Through your sincere involvement in phonetic challenges, you become a linguistic acrobat, a phonetic virtuoso, and a testament to the profound influence of sounds on our language expression, cultural understanding, and the joy of linguistic play. Each tongue twister you master becomes a testament to your linguistic journey, a symphony of sounds that captivates and entertains, and a reflection of the enduring impact of phonetic mastery on our interconnected world of language.

In your consistent pursuit of phonetic and linguistic wanderlust, may each tongue twister you tackle be a celebration of linguistic diversity, an embodiment of your dedication to mastering sounds, and a testament to the lasting impact of communication in shaping our language skills, fostering linguistic curiosity, and creating a world united by the joy of playful language.

Cultivating Phonetic Proficiency and Creative Expression

To further enhance your "Language Play" experience and cultivate phonetic proficiency and creative expression, consider these practical strategies:

1. Phonetic Games: Engage in phonetic games. Challenge yourself and friends with phonetic puzzles, anagrams, or wordplay, fostering a playful approach to mastering sounds.

2. Linguistic Art Projects: Create linguistic art. Design visual representations of tongue twisters using calligraphy, typography, or graphic design, merging artistic expression with phonetic mastery.

3. Collaborative Tongue Twister Recordings: Collaborate with fellow learners. Create collaborative tongue twister recordings where each participant contributes a unique twist, showcasing diverse pronunciations.

Transferring Phonetic Mastery Beyond Language

1. Phonetic Storytelling: Craft phonetic narratives. Write short stories or scripts that incorporate tongue twisters, combining storytelling with phonetic mastery.

2. Phonetic Performance: Perform tongue twisters creatively. Combine tongue twisters with gestures, expressions, or acting to transform phonetic challenges into captivating performances.

Boundless Adventure of Language Play

As you traverse the world of "Language Play," reiterate to yourself that your wanderings are an everlasting journey of linguistic ingenuity, creative expression, and linguistic delight. "Tongue Twisters and Challenges" signify not just tongue gymnastics, but a lifelong commitment to refining sounds, embracing linguistic play, and fostering a deeper connection to language.

By becoming a part of phonetic challenges, you become a linguistic artist, a creative wordsmith, and a testament to the enduring influence of sounds on our language expression, artistic endeavors, and the joy of linguistic exploration. Each tongue twister you conquer becomes a testament to your linguistic journey, a brushstroke that adds vibrancy to language, and a reflection of the enduring impact of phonetic proficiency on our interconnected world of expression.

In your continuous pursuit of phonetic and linguistic flight, may each tongue twister you conquer be a celebration of linguistic artistry, an embodiment of your dedication to mastering sounds, and a testament to the lasting impact of creative expression in shaping our language skills, fostering linguistic curiosity, and creating a world united by the playful beauty of language.

CHAPTER 38

Storytelling Secrets: Crafting Your Story - From Idea to Narration

Welcome to a captivating voyage of imagination and linguistic prowess through "Storytelling Secrets." In this chapter, we set out on a journey to attain a thrilling exploration of the art of storytelling, guiding you through the enchanting process of creating narratives from inception to narration. "Crafting Your Story" is not just about weaving tales; it's a key to harnessing your creativity, enhancing language skills, and captivating audiences with the power of narrative. Through this learning-oriented ramble, you'll unlock the secrets of storytelling, nurture your imagination, and open the door to an opportunity to a journey that melds language and artistry.

Make preparations for the onset of a pilgrimage on an unforgettable adventure of storytelling mastery.

The Essence of "Storytelling Secrets": Unveiling Creative Language

1. Narrative Prowess: "Storytelling Secrets" celebrates the art of narration. By occupying oneself in the storytelling process, you refine your ability to structure narratives, evoke emotions, and communicate effectively.

2. Language Craftsmanship: Just as stories unfold, crafting tales enhances language craftsmanship. Embracing "Crafting Your Story" empowers you to express ideas eloquently and captivate audiences through the magic of storytelling.

Navigating Story Creation: Unveiling "Crafting Your Story"

1. Idea Exploration: Dive into the realm of imagination. Explore techniques for generating ideas, themes, and concepts that lay the foundation for compelling narratives.

2. Structuring the Plot: Develop a solid narrative structure. Learn how to create engaging beginnings, build tension

through rising action, and bring resolutions to life in your stories.

Cultural Insights Through "Storytelling Secrets"

1. Cultural Storytelling Traditions: Discover cultural storytelling traditions. Explore how different cultures use narratives to convey morals, preserve history, and entertain, gaining insights into global storytelling diversity.

2. Themes and Values: Recognize cultural themes and values in stories. Analyze how storytelling reflects cultural beliefs, societal norms, and the human experience across different languages and traditions.

"Crafting Your Story" in Action: Narration and Expression

1. Narrative Voice Development: Develop your narrative voice. Experiment with different tones, perspectives, and styles to infuse your storytelling with unique character and expression.

2. Descriptive Language Mastery: Master descriptive language. Practice using vivid imagery, metaphors, and

sensory details to bring settings, characters, and emotions to life in your stories.

Language Enhancement Through "Storytelling Secrets"

1. Literary Analysis: Hone your critical thinking. Analyze literary techniques in stories written in Mandarin, exploring how authors use language to convey meaning and emotion.

2. Vocabulary Expansion: Expand your vocabulary through storytelling. Integrate new words, idioms, and expressions into your narratives, enriching your language repertoire.

"Crafting Your Story" in Action: Storytelling Platforms

1. Digital Storytelling: Embrace digital mediums. Create multimedia stories using text, images, audio, or video, enhancing your storytelling skills while exploring digital creativity.

2. Oral Storytelling Performance: Engage in oral storytelling. Present your stories to an audience, practicing clear enunciation, expressive delivery, and engaging narration.

Practical Application and Creative Expression

1. Storytelling Workshops: Facilitate storytelling workshops. Share your storytelling insights with language learners, guiding them through the process of crafting their own narratives.

2. Multilingual Storytelling: Craft stories in multiple languages. Compare and contrast storytelling techniques and linguistic nuances, fostering cross-linguistic storytelling expertise.

Learning Beyond "Storytelling Secrets": Global Narratives

1. Cultural Storytelling Exchange: Collaborate on cultural storytelling projects. Work with storytellers from different cultures to create multilingual story collections, celebrating diverse narratives.

2. Adaptation and Translation: Adapt stories across languages. Translate your stories into Mandarin or other languages, exploring how narrative elements are conveyed in different linguistic contexts.

Continued Storytelling Mastery and Linguistic Exploration

As you journey through the world of "Storytelling Secrets," remember that your adventure is an ongoing exploration of creative expression, narrative artistry, and linguistic innovation. "Crafting Your Story" signifies not just narrative construction, but a lifelong commitment to nurturing your imagination, refining your language skills, and connecting with audiences through the timeless magic of storytelling.

By becoming deeply involved in storytelling, you become a wordsmith, a cultural ambassador, and a testament to the profound influence of narratives on our language expression, cross-cultural understanding, and the beauty of human connection. Each story you craft becomes a testament to your linguistic journey, a narrative thread that weaves through cultures and languages, and a reflection of the enduring impact of storytelling mastery on our interconnected world of expression.

As your journey unfolds storytelling and linguistic itinerary, may each narrative you create be a celebration of creativity, an embodiment of your dedication to crafting stories, and a testament to the lasting impact of communication in shaping our language skills, fostering literary appreciation, and creating a world united by the art of storytelling.

Cultivating Storytelling Mastery and Creative Expression

To further enhance your "Storytelling Secrets" experience and cultivate storytelling mastery and creative expression, consider these practical strategies:

1. Interactive Storytelling Workshops: Lead interactive workshops. Organize storytelling sessions where participants collaborate to craft stories in Mandarin, fostering a supportive and creative environment.

2. Multimedia Storytelling Projects: Create multimedia narratives. Develop digital storytelling projects that incorporate text, visuals, audio, and video, experimenting with diverse storytelling mediums.

3. Story Analysis Book Club: Form a story analysis book club. Read and discuss Mandarin literature, dissecting narrative techniques, character development, and thematic exploration.

Transferring Storytelling Skills Beyond Language

1. Cultural Story Adaptation: Adapt stories from different cultures. Rewrite and adapt stories from other languages into

Mandarin, exploring how narratives can be transformed while retaining their essence.

2. Cross-Linguistic Storytelling: Collaborate with multilingual storytellers. Work together to create stories that seamlessly transition between Mandarin and other languages, celebrating linguistic diversity.

Evergreen Odyssey of Storytelling Mastery

As you continue to traverse the world of "Storytelling Secrets," remind yourself that your quest is a perpetual journey of creative ingenuity, cultural understanding, and the timeless magic of storytelling. "Crafting Your Story" signifies not just narrative artistry, but an enduring commitment to harnessing your imagination, honing your storytelling skills, and forging deeper connections through the captivating power of tales.

By becoming earnestly committed to storytelling, you become a literary artisan, a narrative weaver, and a testament to the profound influence of stories on our language expression, cultural appreciation, and the art of human connection. Each story you craft becomes a testament to your linguistic journey, a brushstroke that adds colors to the canvas of human experience, and a reflection of the enduring impact of storytelling on our interconnected world of expression.

Amid your unchanging storytelling and linguistic flight, may each narrative you create be a celebration of creativity, an embodiment of your dedication to storytelling mastery, and a testament to the lasting impact of communication in shaping our language skills, fostering literary appreciation, and creating a world united by the timeless beauty of storytelling.

CHAPTER 39

Cultural Crafts: Exploring Chinese Writing - Creative Calligraphy

Welcome to a captivating exploration of artistic expression and linguistic elegance through "Cultural Crafts." In this chapter, we start a quest for a fascinating journey into the world of Chinese calligraphy, delving into the intricate art of writing that has adorned Chinese culture for centuries. "Creative Calligraphy" is not just about strokes and characters; it's a pathway to appreciating the beauty of Chinese script, enhancing your visual and fine motor skills, and immersing yourself in the rich cultural heritage of writing. Through this learning-oriented expedition, you'll unveil the secrets of calligraphy, nurture your creativity, and enter upon a voyage that fuses art and language. Prepare to set forth on an unforgettable adventure into the realm of Chinese writing.

The Essence of "Cultural Crafts": Embracing Artistic Language

1. Artful Expression: "Cultural Crafts" celebrates the artistry of culture. By involving oneself in calligraphy, you not only refine your writing skills but also express your creativity through a visually captivating medium.

2. Cultural Appreciation: Just as art transcends, cultural crafts deepen your connection. Embracing "Creative Calligraphy" empowers you to appreciate the aesthetics of Chinese writing and the cultural significance it hol

Navigating Chinese Calligraphy: Unveiling "Creative Calligraphy"

1. Writing Styles: Dive into diverse writing styles. Explore the elegance of regular script, the dynamism of cursive script, and the classic beauty of seal script, discovering the nuances of each style.

2. Strokes and Structure: Master the art of strokes. Learn fundamental brushstrokes, their order, and the structure of characters, honing your precision and control.

Cultural Insights Through "Creative Calligraphy"

1. Historical Significance: Discover the historical role of calligraphy. Explore how Chinese calligraphy has preserved literature, conveyed wisdom, and served as a cultural emblem across generations.

2. Symbolism and Aesthetics: Recognize the symbolism and aesthetics in calligraphy. Analyze how brushstrokes and character forms evoke emotions, reflect cultural values, and contribute to the visual harmony of writing.

"Creative Calligraphy" in Action: Visual Expression and Artistry

1. Character Practice: Develop character mastery. Practice writing characters, focusing on stroke order, balance, and rhythm to create visually appealing and authentic calligraphy.

2. Composition Design: Design compositions. Experiment with arranging characters on paper, considering spacing,

proportions, and artistic arrangement to create aesthetically pleasing calligraphic works.

Language Enhancement Through "Cultural Crafts"

1. Character Interpretation: Deepen your character understanding. Study the meanings and origins of characters as you practice calligraphy, connecting linguistic knowledge to visual artistry.

2. Bilingual Calligraphy: Engage in bilingual calligraphy. Write phrases or sentences in both Mandarin and your native language, exploring how calligraphy bridges linguistic boundaries.

"Creative Calligraphy" in Action: Artistic Showcases

1. Calligraphic Projects: Create calligraphic projects. Craft personalized art pieces, bookmarks, or greeting cards adorned with your calligraphy, infusing your creations with cultural charm.

2. Exhibition Participation: Showcase your calligraphy. Participate in local art exhibitions or cultural events, sharing your calligraphic works and sparking conversations about language and art.

Practical Application and Cultural Appreciation

1. Calligraphy Workshops: Host calligraphy workshops. Share your calligraphy skills with others, guiding participants in exploring the beauty of Chinese writing.

2. Cultural Craft Collaborations: Collaborate with artists. Combine calligraphy with other art forms, such as painting or sculpture, to create multidisciplinary cultural crafts.

Learning Beyond "Cultural Crafts": Global Artistry

1. Cross-Cultural Calligraphy Fusion: Fuse calligraphy styles. Experiment with blending Chinese calligraphy with artistic elements from other cultures, creating a unique cross-cultural art form.

2. Multilingual Script Exploration: Study script diversity. Compare Chinese calligraphy with other writing systems, analyzing how different scripts convey meaning and aesthetics.

Continued Cultural Exploration and Artistic Discovery

As you journey through the world of "Cultural Crafts," remember that your adventure is an ongoing exploration of artistic expression, cultural enrichment, and visual storytelling. "Creative Calligraphy" signifies not just brush and ink, but a lifelong commitment to appreciating art, refining your skills, and fostering a deeper connection to cultural heritage.

By contributing to calligraphy, you become an artist, a cultural ambassador, and a testament to the profound influence of visual language on our artistic expression, cross-cultural understanding, and the celebration of human creativity. Each calligraphic work you create becomes a testament to your artistic journey, a stroke that conveys meaning and beauty, and a reflection of the enduring impact of calligraphy on our interconnected world of artistic interpretation.

As you persist in your pursuit of calligraphic and artistic cruise, may each stroke you make be a celebration of creativity, an embodiment of your dedication to calligraphy, and a testament to the lasting impact of artistic expression in shaping our appreciation for culture, fostering visual beauty, and creating a world united by the art of writing.

Cultivating Artistic Mastery and Cultural Connection

To further enhance your "Cultural Crafts" experience and cultivate artistic mastery and cultural connection, consider these practical strategies:

1. Digital Calligraphy Tools: Explore digital calligraphy. Experiment with digital platforms or tablet apps that simulate brush and ink, combining traditional techniques with modern technology.

2. Collaborative Calligraphy Projects: Collaborate with fellow artists. Create joint calligraphy projects where each participant contributes a unique character or element, fostering artistic exchange.

3. Cultural Calligraphy Exchanges: Engage in cultural calligraphy exchanges. Connect with calligraphers from Mandarin-speaking regions, sharing insights and learning about different calligraphy traditions.

Transferring Artistic Skills Beyond Language

1. Multilingual Calligraphy Fusion: Merge calligraphy with other languages. Write calligraphy pieces that incorporate characters from multiple languages, celebrating linguistic diversity.

2. Cultural Craft Showcase: Organize cultural craft exhibitions. Curate an art show that highlights calligraphy alongside other cultural crafts, promoting cross-cultural appreciation.

Unending Safari of Artistic Exploration

As you persevere in your exploration of "Cultural Crafts," remember that your journey is a continuous pursuit of artistic expression, cultural preservation, and the profound impact of visual language. "Creative Calligraphy" signifies not just strokes on paper, but an ongoing commitment to embracing beauty, refining your artistry, and connecting with the cultural legacy of calligraphy.

Through your wholehearted involvement in calligraphy, you become a visual poet, a cultural interpreter, and a testament to the enduring influence of art on our visual communication, cross-cultural understanding, and the appreciation of human creativity. Each calligraphic creation you bring to life becomes a testament to your artistic journey, a brushstroke that conveys emotions and stories, and a reflection of the lasting impact of calligraphy on our interconnected world of visual interpretation.

In your committed journey towards artistic and calligraphic excellence, may each stroke you master be a celebration of artistic craftsmanship, an embodiment of your dedication to calligraphy, and a testament to the lasting impact of artistic expression in shaping our appreciation for culture, fostering visual beauty, and creating a world united by the mesmerizing art of writing.

CHAPTER 40

Tea Time Tales:
Conversations Over Tea

Step into the serene world of "Tea Time Tales," where the aromatic embrace of tea serves as the backdrop for captivating conversations. In this chapter, we take the first steps in a soothing journey of social interaction and cultural exchange, exploring the art of sharing stories, ideas, and experiences over a cup of tea. "Sip and Share" is not just about the beverage; it's a gateway to meaningful connections, enhancing communication skills, and immersing oneself in the rich tapestry of tea culture. Through this learning-oriented escapade, you'll uncover the essence of tea as a catalyst for dialogue, nurture your social abilities, and embark on an intimate voyage of cultural appreciation. Get your act together to savor the experience of "Tea Time Tales."

The Essence of "Tea Time Tales": Cultivating Connection

1. Social Bonding: "Tea Time Tales" celebrates the art of connection. By engaging in conversations over tea, you foster interpersonal relationships and cultivate the ability to engage meaningfully.

2. Cultural Exploration: Just as tea transcends borders, tea time is a portal to culture. Embracing "Sip and Share" allows you to delve into tea rituals, etiquette, and the cultural significance of tea across societies.

Navigating Tea Conversations: Unveiling "Sip and Share"

1. Tea Varieties: Dive into the world of teas. Explore different types of tea, their flavors, and the cultural contexts in which they are enjoyed, broadening your understanding of tea culture.

2. Tea Rituals: Master the art of tea preparation. Learn about the traditional methods of brewing tea, the significance of each step, and the rituals associated with different tea cultures.

Cultural Insights Through "Sip and Share"

1. Tea Across Cultures: Discover tea's global appeal. Explore how tea has been an integral part of various cultures, representing hospitality, relaxation, and social harmony.

2. Tea Etiquette: Recognize the nuances of tea etiquette. Analyze how different cultures approach tea conversations, including serving rituals, gestures, and customary behaviors.

"Sip and Share" in Action: Engaging Conversations

1. Storytelling Over Tea: Share personal anecdotes. Engage in storytelling while sipping tea, fostering a cozy atmosphere for sharing experiences, memories, and emotions.

2. Cultural Exchange: Embrace cross-cultural dialogue. Connect with others from Mandarin-speaking regions, sharing insights about tea customs and exchanging stories about its role in daily life.

Language Enhancement Through "Tea Time Tales"

1. Vocabulary Expansion: Learn tea-related vocabulary. Integrate specialized terms into your conversations, enhancing your language skills while discussing tea varieties, preparation, and experiences.

2. Conversational Fluency: Enhance your conversational fluency. Practice discussing tea topics in Mandarin, refining your ability to express preferences, opinions, and observations.

"Sip and Share" in Action: Tea Gatherings

1. Tea Tasting Gatherings: Host tea tastings. Organize gatherings where participants sample different teas, share their impressions, and engage in discussions about flavor profiles.

2. Cultural Tea Experiences: Attend cultural tea events. Participate in tea ceremonies, workshops, or events that offer hands-on experiences with tea preparation and conversation.

Practical Application and Cultural Appreciation

1. Tea Conversation Circles: Form tea conversation groups. Establish regular meetups where participants discuss various topics over tea, fostering a supportive and culturally enriching environment.

2. Cultural Culinary Collaborations: Collaborate on cultural culinary projects. Combine tea conversations with culinary

endeavors, such as preparing tea-infused dishes, exploring the intersection of food and culture.

Learning Beyond "Tea Time Tales": Global Connections

1. Virtual Tea Exchanges: Engage in virtual tea gatherings. Connect with individuals from different regions online, sharing tea experiences and cultural insights virtually.

2. Tea and Language Fusion: Merge tea with language learning. Study Mandarin while exploring tea culture, creating a unique fusion of language education and cultural immersion.

Continued Cultural Connection and Conversational Flourishing

As you journey through the world of "Tea Time Tales," remember that your adventure is an ongoing exploration of connection, cultural understanding, and the delightful conversations inspired by tea. "Sip and Share" signifies not just a beverage, but a lifelong commitment to nurturing relationships, refining your communication skills, and embracing the shared pleasure of tea.

Through your sincere commitment to tea conversations, you become a cultural ambassador, a convivial host, and a testament to the enduring influence of shared experiences on our interpersonal relationships, cross-cultural appreciation, and the warmth of human connection. Each cup of tea you share becomes a testament to your journey, a vessel for stories and laughter, and a reflection of the lasting impact of meaningful conversations on our interconnected world of dialogue.

As you press forward on your tea-infused journey, may each sip you take be a celebration of camaraderie, an embodiment of your dedication to connecting through tea, and a testament to the enduring impact of conversations in shaping our relationships, fostering cultural appreciation, and creating a world united by the art of sharing stories over a cup of tea.

Cultivating Cultural Connection and Conversational Excellence

To further enhance your "Tea Time Tales" experience and cultivate cultural connection and conversational excellence, consider these practical strategies:

1. Tea Exchange Programs: Participate in tea exchange programs. Connect with individuals from Mandarin-speaking regions for virtual tea sessions, exchanging insights about tea culture and daily life.

2. Tea Travel Adventures: Embark upon a mission to tea-related travel. Visit tea-producing regions to immerse yourself in local tea traditions, engage in conversations with tea experts, and deepen your understanding of tea culture.

3. Multilingual Tea Gatherings: Organize multilingual tea gatherings. Host events where participants converse in Mandarin, English, and other languages, creating a dynamic language exchange centered around tea.

Transferring Conversational Skills Beyond Language

1. Culinary Language Fusion: Combine tea with culinary experiences. Engage in conversations about food, flavors, and cultural dishes while enjoying tea, merging language learning with culinary exploration.

2. Tea and Art Collaboration: Collaborate with artists. Partner with visual artists or writers to create tea-inspired artworks, stories, or poetry, blending language and art in unique ways.

A Lifelong Journey of Cultural Connection

While you move forward with your exploration of "Tea Time Tales," remember that your journey is an ongoing endeavor of fostering connections, embracing cultural diversity, and the timeless joy of conversing over tea. "Sip and Share" signifies not just a fleeting interaction, but a commitment to building bridges, refining your communication skills, and cherishing the bonds that form over shared moments.

By becoming actively engaged in tea conversations, you become a cultural enthusiast, a storyteller, and a testament to the enduring influence of conversations on our understanding of different cultures, cross-cultural harmony, and the beauty of human interaction. Each cup of tea you enjoy becomes a testament to your journey, a vessel for cultural exchange, and a reflection of the lasting impact of meaningful dialogues on our interconnected world of relationships.

During your unwavering commitment to tea-infused voyage, may each conversation you have be a celebration of shared experiences, an embodiment of your dedication to cultural connection, and a testament to the lasting impact of conversational excellence in shaping our appreciation for diverse perspectives, fostering meaningful interactions, and creating a world united by the simple pleasure of sharing stories and ideas over a cup of tea.

CHAPTER 41

Learning Exchange: Connecting with Native Speakers - Language Swap

Step into a realm of interactive and immersive language learning in "Learning Exchange." In this chapter, we step onto the path of an exciting journey of linguistic and cultural exploration through the concept of "Language Swap." This immersive experience takes language learning to a new level by connecting you with native speakers, allowing you to practice, exchange, and absorb language in its natural context. "Language Swap" is not just about words; it's a pathway to building meaningful connections, enhancing language skills, and immersing yourself in the rich tapestry of global cultures. Through this learning-oriented adventure, you'll unlock the power of authentic conversations, nurture your communication abilities, and initiate a pursuit of an enriching voyage of intercultural understanding. Ready yourself mentally to engage in the transformative practice of "Learning Exchange."

The Essence of "Learning Exchange": Cultural and Linguistic Fusion

1. Interactive Learning: "Learning Exchange" celebrates the art of interactive learning. By getting into language swaps, you transcend traditional textbooks and immerse yourself in authentic language usage.

2. Cultural Exchange: Just as languages connect, "Language Swap" is a gateway to cultural connection. Embracing this practice allows you to explore diverse perspectives, customs, and lifestyles.

Navigating Language Swaps: Unveiling "Language Swap"

1. Native Speaker Partnerships: Connect with native speakers. Seek language partners from Mandarin-speaking regions to initiate language swaps, cultivating an environment of mutual learning.

2. Conversational Themes: Choose diverse topics. Explore a range of subjects, from daily life and hobbies to cultural insights, fostering engaging and insightful conversations.

Cultural Insights Through "Language Swap"

1. Cultural Nuances: Discover cultural nuances. Engage in discussions about customs, traditions, and societal norms, gaining a deeper understanding of the cultural context in which the language is used.

2. Idiomatic Expressions: Learn idiomatic expressions. Exchange idioms and colloquial phrases unique to the language, enhancing your conversational fluency and cultural integration.

"Language Swap" in Action: Immersive Conversations

1. Language Immersion: Dive into authentic contexts. Practice language in real-life scenarios, such as ordering food, making travel plans, or discussing current events, replicating the immersive experience of living in a Mandarin-speaking environment.

2. Cultural Show and Tell: Share cultural insights. Introduce your partner to your culture while learning about theirs, facilitating cross-cultural dialogue and mutual appreciation.

Language Enhancement Through "Learning Exchange"

1. Vocabulary Enrichment: Expand your vocabulary. Learn new words, phrases, and expressions in context, building a dynamic vocabulary that reflects everyday language usage.

2. Accent and Pronunciation: Refine your accent. Receive feedback from native speakers, improving your pronunciation and intonation for more authentic communication.

"Language Swap" in Action: Interactive Learning

1. Cultural Exchange Projects: Collaborate on cultural projects. Choose a topic of mutual interest, such as cooking, music, or art, and create joint projects that celebrate both languages and cultures.

2. Language Exchange Events: Participate in language exchange events. Attend local language swap meetups or virtual gatherings, where participants converse in Mandarin and other languages, promoting linguistic diversity.

Practical Application and Cultural Enrichment

1. Language Swap Networks: Join language swap networks. Connect with language enthusiasts worldwide, engaging in virtual language swaps that span continents and cultures.

2. Cultural Exchange Workshops: Lead cultural workshops. Share insights about your culture or Mandarin-speaking regions, facilitating cultural exchange while practicing language skills.

Learning Beyond "Learning Exchange": Lifelong Connections

1. Cross-Cultural Friendships: Foster cross-cultural friendships. Develop lasting bonds with your language partners, creating relationships that transcend language learning and contribute to your global network.

2. Multilingual Dialogue Fusion: Merge multiple languages. Engage in multilingual conversations, where participants switch between Mandarin and other languages, celebrating linguistic diversity and global connections.

Continued Linguistic and Cultural Exploration

Amidst your ongoing dedication to journey through "Learning Exchange," remember that your adventure is an ongoing exploration of linguistic growth, cultural enrichment, and the transformative power of authentic communication. "Language Swap" signifies not just words exchanged, but a lifelong commitment to building bridges, refining communication skills, and cherishing the connections formed through language.

By actively participating in language swaps, you become a cultural ambassador, a global communicator, and a testament to the enduring influence of cross-cultural connections on our linguistic proficiency, intercultural awareness, and the beauty of human interaction. Each conversation you share becomes a testament to your journey, a bridge between languages, and a reflection of the lasting impact of meaningful dialogue on our interconnected world of relationships.

In your relentless linguistic voyage, may each language swap you engage in be a celebration of diverse voices, an embodiment of your dedication to authentic communication, and a testament to the lasting impact of linguistic and cultural exchange in shaping our appreciation for global perspectives, fostering meaningful interactions, and creating a world united by the art of language and connection.

Cultivating Linguistic Proficiency and Cultural Bonds

To intensify the enrichment of your "Learning Exchange" experience and cultivate linguistic proficiency and cultural bonds, consider these practical strategies:

1. Cultural Immersion Trips: Plan cultural immersion trips. Visit Mandarin-speaking regions to engage in face-to-face language swaps, allowing you to experience local culture and language firsthand.

2. Virtual Cultural Events: Attend virtual cultural events. Participate in online cultural festivals, workshops, or presentations organized by native speakers, deepening your cultural understanding.

3. Language Swap Clubs: Form language swap clubs. Establish local or online clubs where members can connect for regular language swaps, providing a consistent platform for language practice.

Transferring Linguistic Skills Beyond Language

1. Cultural Collaborative Projects: Collaborate with language partners on creative projects. Write short stories, create videos, or design presentations together, fostering artistic expression while practicing language.

2. Cultural Cuisine Exchanges: Organize cultural cuisine exchanges. Share traditional recipes with your language partner and learn how to prepare dishes from their culture, merging language and culinary exploration.

A Lifelong Journey of Linguistic Exploration

During your tireless exploration of "Learning Exchange," remember that your journey is an ongoing voyage of linguistic development, cultural enrichment, and the profound impact of authentic communication. "Language Swap" signifies not just words spoken, but an enduring commitment to fostering understanding, honing language skills, and cherishing the bonds that transcend language barriers.

Via your dedicated participation in language swaps, you become a language enthusiast, a cultural collaborator, and a testament to the enduring influence of authentic dialogue on our linguistic competence, cross-cultural harmony, and the beauty of human connection. Each conversation you initiate becomes a testament to your journey, a bridge between cultures, and a reflection of the lasting impact of meaningful communication on our interconnected world of relationships.

Throughout your steady linguistic journey, may each language swap you undertake be a celebration of shared knowledge, an embodiment of your dedication to cross-cultural understanding, and a testament to the lasting impact of linguistic and cultural exchange in shaping our appreciation for diverse cultures, fostering authentic connections, and creating a world united by the art of language and mutual learning.

CHAPTER 42

Future Footsteps: Continuing Your Mandarin Journey

Step into the realm of possibilities as we embark on the final chapter of your Mandarin voyage, "Future Footsteps." Here, we explore in greater detail the exciting prospects that lie ahead on your ongoing journey to master Mandarin. As you conclude your comprehensive exploration, you'll discover how to continue nurturing your language skills, engaging with cultural insights, and expanding your horizons beyond the pages of this guide. "Next Chapter Awaits" is not just a conclusion; it's a gateway to lifelong learning, cultural enrichment, and the limitless potential of your Mandarin crossing. Through this learning-oriented culmination, you'll gain insights on sustaining language proficiency, staying culturally connected, and embracing the endless possibilities that await you. Get yourself in place to step confidently into the future of your Mandarin journey.

Transitioning to Future Success: Sustaining Proficiency

1. Consistent Practice: Maintain regular practice. Set aside dedicated time for language activities, whether it's daily conversations, reading materials, or watching Mandarin media.

2. Language Apps and Resources: Utilize language apps. Continue using language learning apps and online resources to reinforce your skills, expand your vocabulary, and practice pronunciation.

Cultural Enrichment Beyond the Guide: Staying Connected

1. Cultural Events and Festivals: Attend cultural events. Participate in local or virtual events celebrating Mandarin culture, such as festivals, exhibitions, and performances.

2. Cultural Organizations: Join cultural groups. Become a member of local or online cultural organizations focused on

Mandarin-speaking communities, allowing you to engage with native speakers and cultural enthusiasts.

Expanding Horizons: Embracing New Opportunities

1. Advanced Language Courses: Enroll in advanced courses. Pursue higher-level language courses or specialized programs to deepen your linguistic understanding and proficiency.

2. Cultural Immersion Travel: Plan cultural immersion trips. Visit Mandarin-speaking regions to experience authentic culture, refine your language skills, and build lasting connections

Continuing Your Language Learning Journey: Lifelong Growth

1. Language Learning Communities: Join language learning communities. Participate in forums, social media groups, or local meetups where learners share experiences, insights, and resources.

2. Language Teaching: Share your knowledge. Consider teaching Mandarin to beginners or offering language exchange opportunities to continue practicing and teaching.

Cultural Exploration Beyond the Guide: Lifelong Connection

1. Cultural Exploration Projects: Initiate cultural projects. Engage in research, writing, or creative endeavors that explore specific aspects of Mandarin culture, fostering ongoing cultural appreciation.

2. Cultural Collaboration: Collaborate with native speakers. Partner with Mandarin speakers on joint projects, such as language exchange, cultural presentations, or creative works.

Charting Your Personal Path: Lifelong Learning

1. Goal Setting: Set new language goals. Define objectives for your Mandarin journey, whether it's achieving fluency, passing language exams, or engaging in advanced conversations.

2. Mentorship and Guidance: Seek mentorship. Connect with experienced Mandarin learners or native speakers who can provide guidance, support, and insights for your continued growth.

Learning Beyond the Guide: Your Journey Continues

As you step into the future with "Future Footsteps," remember that your journey is a continuation of discovery, growth, and the unwavering pursuit of excellence in Mandarin. "Next Chapter Awaits" signifies not just an end, but a new beginning—a testament to your commitment to lifelong learning, cultural enrichment, and the profound impact of mastering a language.

Through your engagement with "Future Footsteps," you become a lifelong learner, a cultural ambassador, and a testament to the enduring influence of curiosity, dedication, and the pursuit of knowledge. Each step you take becomes a testament to your journey, a progression towards linguistic and cultural mastery, and a reflection of the lasting impact of continuous growth on our interconnected world of personal development.

In the process of your Mandarin trip, may each new chapter you embrace be a celebration of progress, an embodiment of your dedication to learning, and a testament to the lasting impact of education in shaping our understanding of languages, cultures, and the boundless possibilities that await us.

Embracing Cultural and Linguistic Horizons

For heightened augmentation of your "Future Footsteps" experience and cultivate continuous growth and exploration, consider these practical strategies:

1. Language Challenges: Engage in language challenges. Participate in language-learning challenges online or create your own to keep your skills sharp and maintain motivation.

2. Cultural Exchanges: Foster cultural exchanges. Collaborate with Mandarin-speaking friends or language partners to organize cultural exchange events, where you share your culture and learn about theirs.

3. Language Immersion Retreats: Attend language immersion retreats. Join immersive language programs or retreats in Mandarin-speaking regions, providing intensive language practice and cultural immersion.

Transferring Knowledge Beyond the Guide

1. Language Teaching Platforms: Teach others. Utilize language teaching platforms to offer online lessons, sharing your knowledge and helping others on their Mandarin learning journey.

2. Bilingual Content Creation: Create bilingual content. Start a blog, podcast, or YouTube channel where you share language and culture-related content, building a platform for cultural exchange and language learning.

Continuing the Journey of Lifelong Learning

1. Advanced Language Study: Pursue advanced studies. Enroll in advanced language programs, linguistics courses, or cultural studies to deepen your understanding and expertise.

2. Language Research: Engage in linguistic research. Explore specific linguistic aspects of Mandarin, such as idiomatic expressions, slang, or regional variations, contributing to linguistic scholarship.

Charting Your Personal Path: Embracing Growth

1. Cultural Ambassadorship: Promote cultural understanding. Advocate for cross-cultural appreciation by organizing cultural events, workshops, or initiatives that promote understanding and harmony.

2. Cultural Integration: Immerse in local culture. Seek opportunities to integrate Mandarin into your daily life, from

reading news and books to engaging with Mandarin-speaking communities.

Learning Beyond "Future Footsteps": A Lifelong Voyage

As you step boldly into the future with "Future Footsteps," remember that your journey is boundless—a testament to your determination to never stop learning, growing, and connecting. "Next Chapter Awaits" signifies not just the end of a guide, but the beginning of an ongoing narrative—a testament to your dedication to expanding your horizons, enriching your understanding, and the enduring impact of continuous learning.

Through your embrace of "Future Footsteps," you become a lifelong explorer, a cultural bridge, and a testament to the timeless value of education, personal development, and the limitless rewards of cultivating a multilingual and culturally enriched life. Each step you take becomes a testament to your journey, an evolution of your linguistic and cultural prowess, and a reflection of the lasting impact of dedication to lifelong learning on our interconnected world of knowledge and growth.

In the progression of your Mandarin journey, may each new chapter you unfold be a celebration of curiosity, an embodiment of your dedication to exploration, and a testament to the enduring impact of learning in shaping our perspectives, fostering cultural connections, and creating a world united by the beauty of language, culture, and lifelong discovery.

ABOUT THE AUTHOR

Zhang Y. Hua is a visionary educator and linguist at the forefront of transforming Mandarin Chinese language instruction. With a profound commitment to making language learning accessible and enjoyable, Zhang Y. Hua has crafted a unique approach that goes beyond traditional methods. His book, "Chitchat Chronicles: A Beginner's Guide to Mandarin Chinese with Short Stories and Accent Mastery," exemplifies his dedication to empowering learners and fostering cross-cultural communication.

Zhang Y. Hua's academic journey is marked by a deep passion for language and intercultural exchange. Armed with advanced degrees in Applied Linguistics and Language Teaching, he possesses a solid foundation in linguistic theory while keeping a keen eye on practical pedagogy. His extensive teaching experience spans across diverse learner backgrounds and proficiency levels, affirming her versatility as an educator.

"Chitchat Chronicles" stands as a testament to Zhang Y. Hua